OUR BUSINESS
CIVILIZATION

☆ B O N I B O O K S ☆

OUR BUSINESS CIVILIZATION

☆

*Some Aspects
of American Culture*

BY

JAMES TRUSLOW ADAMS

☆ ALBERT & CHARLES BONI ☆

917.3
Ad1o

21968
Sept '46

TO KAY

PREFACE

All of the chapters included in this volume have appeared in various magazines, although in their present form many of them have been altered and several of them have been greatly enlarged. The author wishes emphatically to state that the volume is not intended to give a fair and complete presentation of the contemporary American scene and its tendencies. The essays deal only with certain aspects, as the title of the book indicates, and those the more sinister ones now to be noted in what is, in many respects, the vigorous growth of our national life. If a doctor pronounces a patient to have a bad circulation and a dangerous local infection in his leg, it cannot be complained of him that he has failed to speak the whole truth because he has said nothing of what a good husband, loyal friend and able executive the patient happens to be. Those are not aspects with which the doctor has, at the moment, concerned himself. To change the metaphor, much of the criticism that these essays have encountered when in magazine form, and much of what I confidently anticipate they will now encounter in their new and more elaborate presentation, is based on no more logical ground of attack than that instead of sayng what a dull dish prunes make or how unhealthful cucumbers may be, I should have performed a much more useful, patriotic and agreeable service by saying how delicious strawberries are. My only answer to that sort of criticism is that at the moment I am talking about prunes and cucumbers, not strawberries, though some time I may discuss those. Sufficient unto the day. . .

My thanks are due to the editors of *Harper's Monthly*, the *Atlantic Monthly*, the *Forum*, the *Saturday Review of Literature*, and *McNaught's Monthly*, who enabled me first to discuss my unpopular topics in their pages.

JAMES TRUSLOW ADAMS.

London, 1929.

TABLE OF CONTENTS

CHAPTER I
A BUSINESS MAN'S CIVILIZATION

A BUSINESS MAN'S CIVILIZATION

I

As one grows older and, let us hope, wiser, one becomes more and more shy of easy generalizations and classifications. As one moves through one's world, the old generalized types, for example, of fiction and youth, standing for an "artist," a Frenchman, or an Englishman, break into the many and varying individual artists or Frenchmen or Englishmen of one's acquaintance, much as a ray of white light is broken into a rainbow of colors through a prism. But age and experience would be but poor substitutes for youth and freshness if they resulted only in bringing chaos to our minds, a substitution of multitudinous individuals for species and genus. If the old crude stock-in-trade types compact of ignorance and too facile generalizing have to be submitted to the spectrum of experience, individuals we find, in spite of seemingly baffling variety, do somehow combine to form distinct group types, and in the national sphere character-istics emerge that set one nation off from another even though their millions of inhabitants may differ among them-selves almost more than some of them differ from foreigners. For a traveler constantly passing from one country to another and now long past the stage of mere romantic interest in the exotic, there is no more fascinating task than to attempt to establish the genuine characteristics of a nation out of the welter of individual impressions.

OUR BUSINESS CIVILIZATION

It would be absurd to contend that America offers a simple problem to the observer. If the scene is less varied than in some other countries, nevertheless, to see about one only Babbitts means that one is not an acute observer. But as one comes back again and again from foreign countries, with fresh eyes and new standards of comparison, one comes to simplify our civilization in some respects, as a scientist does the continent. To the lover of scenery the Long Island beaches, the Big Smoky Mountains, the prairies, the Arizona desert, the golden coast of California, or the glaciers of Alaska offer variety in plenty; yet the geologist finds North America the simplest of all the great continents in the basic lines of its structure. In the same way, as we penetrate below the surface variety of its social life, we begin to see that its civilization is equally remarkable as that of the continent itself for its extreme structural simplicity. This simplicity lies in the fact that it has come to be almost wholly a *business man's civilization.*

It may be asked why, in a modern industrial world in which everyone must have money to live, and in which most people are engaged in making it in one way or another, is America any more of a business man's civilization than that of any other country? The answer is to be found in a wide variety of social, economic, historic, geographic, and other factors. Let us, for example, contrast it with England, the country which I know best outside of my own, and where I happen to be writing at the moment. England has always been a great commercial and, for the last century, a great manufacturing country, the "nation of shopkeepers" in the eyes of European continentals. Business and trade are foundation stones of England's prosperity and power, yet English civilization, whatever it may one day become, is not as yet a business man's civilization in the same sense as is America's. The reason is that the influence of the business man here upon society has been limited by the presence of other and very powerful influences stemming from sources other than business and having nothing to do with it.

In the first place, there is that relic of feudalism, the aristocracy, including in its numbers, of course, many men and fortunes made by trade, but exerting its influence through a long tradition. It may be that "every Englishman loves a Lord"—though it is quite certain he does not worship him as do many American women—but it is true that the aristocracy exerts an influence upon the social manners and customs of the people at large which is incomparably greater than that exerted by the probably wealthier, but far less picturesque, untitled bankers, shipping merchants, iron manufacturers, and what not. In the country—still the best source of English life, though fast passing—aristocracy and landed gentry possess so great an influence that if a *nouveau riche* wishes to become somebody, he does not take a great house and give costly entertainments in London but buys an estate somewhere in the "counties" and painfully tries to make his way among families that may have but a fraction of his own wealth.

Nor is the influence of these two great bodies of the aristocracy and gentry based solely on social position or snobbery. Of black sheep in both there have been plenty, but these two classes still retain the best element in the feudal system, the duty of service. The broad lands of the feudal lord, unlike the stocks and bonds of the modern business magnate,

[11]

were not his solely for pleasure. Just as his men owed service to him, so he owed physical protection to them; and he was not likely to retain his lands and castles long if he could not give it. A considerable part of the wealth and power of England is still in the hands of these landowners, large and small, who still perform in more modern ways the duties that go with their wealth. The difference in the sense of responsibility toward the public felt by the descendants of historic families and the members of the new business magnates may be noted in one minor, but illuminating, particular. For the most part the treasures of art accumulated by the old families are regarded by them as a public trust, and the public, at least on certain days of the week are admitted to see them. The private galleries of Knole House, of Warwick Castle and of scores of others are as well known and as easily accessible to the public as are those of the national museums. On the other hand, the motto of the new business magnate is usually "what is mine is my own." As a rule when a picture by a great master is carried through the doors of the palace of a water-power magnate, a meat packer or a banker in America it is lost to the public, save in rare cases as an exhibit in a temporary loan collection, until after long years sale or bequest may bring it into a public museum.

Again, there is the Church of England, dependent for its existence and support not upon the gifts of business men but upon local taxation, age-long endowments, and the support of the State. The leading universities, for similar reasons, are independent of business to an extent impossible in America. Politics, the army, navy, and the diplomatic and civil services offer life-careers for the ablest of men.

The professions, such as law and medicine, are still uncommercialized. A young man of ability and ambition may choose, depending upon his particular tastes or opportunities, among a dozen careers, not one of which has anything to do with business, and any one of which offers him as a possible reward all the prizes that a man can wish, although from the pressure of democracy on the one hand and big business on the other this is becoming less true, perhaps temporarily, than it has been heretofore. However, the successful business man still finds himself only one among many factors influencing the manners, thought, and life of his time. His own contribution is absorbed into the varied and rich life of the nation made up of the ideals and outlook of many other types and classes in addition to his own.

In America from the beginning there has been an entirely different social scene, although in many respects it was more variegated in the seventeenth and eighteenth centuries than it is to-day. Neither the best nor the worst of feudalism, however, was transplanted to the colonies. We fell short of developing an aristocracy or a permanent landed gentry. With the exception of a few colonial experiments, there has never been an established church. Politics, save in a few rare cases, have ceased to attract first-rate men as a career, and there is none either in diplomacy, which is usually only an episode, or in the civil service, which holds no position worth striving for. The rewards of a lifetime spent in the army or navy are negligible. On the other hand, we have the richest virgin continent in the world to exploit, and the prizes for a successful business career, measured in money and power, have been such as are undreamed of in European business. In Europe a "great fortune" is reckoned in millions; in America in hundreds of millions and now, in a few cases, even in billions. Generation after generation the opportunities, instead of becoming less, have become colossally greater. The result has been that most of the energy, ability, and ambition of the country has found its outlet, if not its satisfaction, in business.

Certain results have flowed from this fact. In the first place, human nature alters, perhaps, less than we wish it might. Two of its most persistent traits are love of distinction and the need to follow leaders. When in founding the nation we did away with all titles and badges, we opened the way in a fashion not anticipated to the social sway of the business man. We may note for example that the much-despised stars and ribbons of the old aristocratic order in Europe have been replaced in America, where they are unconstitutional, by the innumerable ornaments of the Mystic Shriners, the Order of Junior Mechanics, and other similar emblems. Theoretically, since the American and French Revolutions men have given lip-service to the doctrine of equality, but in reality everyone craves his own little share of social distinction, a something that will tend to set him somewhat above his neighbor. Founded if you like in vanity, it is, nevertheless, one of the most important elements in progress and conduct.

The great mass of men also tend to copy those above them, those who by common consent are the leaders of the nation, or occupy the most prominent and enviable positions in it. The youth of a savage and warlike tribe will emulate its great warriors and shape his life on theirs. In England, as we have seen, the genuine leaders of the aristocracy and gentry still exert a great influence upon the manners and outlook of those below them. In America these leaders have become the great business men. In their hands are the wealth and power of modern America. Their ideals, their manners, their ways of life, their standard of success are, therefore, those which the great mass of Americans, consciously or not, strive to make their own. In America, moreover, no Order of Merit, no Companionship of the Bath, no peerage is to be won as a symbol of a successful career. Most men, as we have said, crave some badge as a tangible evidence of their distinction if they have attained any. In America for those not content with being a Master of a Grand Lodge or the High Priest of something-or-other wealth is the sole badge of success. All other orders in society having been swept away, and a business career being the sole one that leads inevitably to power when successful, the business man's standard of values has become that of our civilization at large.

Owing in large measure to this, to the emphasis placed in America by our universities on equipment and plant, and to their constant need of money for endowments and upkeep, they also have come under the sway of the successful business men to an extent undreamed of in Europe. If the equipment of European universities seems meager and poor in comparison with America, no one can claim that the work being done in them is inferior; and partly due to the smaller demands for money for constant building and expense, and partly to the presence in the European social system of important classes other than business men, the universities there are far more independent of business domination and ideals than they are with us. The entire religious system of our country, also, is in the same relation of dependence upon the business man. In the absence of any establishment of large endowments from the past, the churches of every denomination are dependent upon the richer members of their congregation for support. As for politics, the relations between parties, legislatures, and the business interests are too notorious to call for specific comment. The present disgraceful struggling of private interest against private interest, with no consideration for the interest of the public or the nation, exhibited in the Tariff controversy in Congress is merely one phase of what we have come to consider a normal relation of American business to American government. The dominant economic and social power of any country is bound to be the dominant political one. If agriculture, for example, is now the Cinderella of American prosperity and government interest, the cause is in part to be found in the fact that the number of men engaged in agriculture has dropped from 90 per cent of the total in 1790 to 36 per cent in 1910 and 29 per cent in 1920. The professions, as we shall note later, are also rapidly coming under the domination of the business man's type of civilization.

Thus, unlike Europe, the business man with us finds himself the dominant power in the life of the nation and almost alone in his control over the direction of its entire life, economic, social, intellectual, religious, and political. It is a situation that, so far as I know, is unique in history and well worth analyzing.

II

First let us analyze the business man himself. Is there such a thing as a business "type"? Thinking of all the variations among those one knows, much as one thinks of one's varied French friends, one may think it impossible classify them under one head; but just, as contrasting one's French friends with English or Russian, a French type does emerge, so contrasting a man who is in business all his life with those engaged in other pursuits, a business type does also take form. Apart from initial tastes and nature, a man is bound to be molded by the aims, ideas, ideals, and whole nature of the career to which he devotes practically his entire energies and time. It is obvious that a poet or musician will react to the facts of existence differently from the way a steel manufacturer, an admiral, a high ecclesiastic, a politician, or a Supreme Court judge would do. All of them naturally have to provide themselves with a living, but the fundamental facts that regulate their reactions to the world about them are different.

For a business man that fundamental fact is, and is bound to be, *profit*. Having made money, the business man may be, as he often is, more generous and careless with it than an aristocrat or a churchman; but that does not alter the fact that the main function of his work, his main preoccupation, and the point from which he views everything connected with his work is that of a profit. For one thing, all men, whether they be poets, soldiers, diplomats, or department-store owners, crave, as we have said, success and recognition in their chosen field. The hallmark of success in business is the extent of profit a man gets out of it. An artist may find no public for his wares but, if he is doing great work, he will be supported by the opinion of his peers. A doctor may struggle in a country village with nothing but a pittance but he has the satisfaction of a noble work nobly done.

A man like Asquith may spend his whole life in the service of his country and yet retire as prime minister with the income of a bank clerk. But a man who spends his life in business and ends no wealthier than he began is voted a failure by all his fellows, even though he may have personal qualities that endear him to his friends.

This fundamental preoccupation with making a profit has been much emphasized by the shift of business from the individual to the corporate form. A man may do what he likes with his own and if he chooses to be quixotic he can be; but in the new triple relationship of workmen, executives, and stockholders in the modern corporation there has ceased to be personality anywhere. The American is a great believer in the magical power of words. The bare facts of business are now being covered over by the new American gospel of "service"; but when we analyze this, does it not merely come down to the obvious facts that the business man performs a highly useful function in society and that, so far as he can, he should see that the public gets its full money's worth? The fundamental need of profit remains. The professional classes—doctors, artists, scholars, scientists and others—may, as they often do, work for little or nothing at all, but, except in the rarest of personal instances, the business man is precluded from doing so. What stockbroker, manufacturing company, railway or electric light corporation with all their talk about service would ever consider running their business at a voluntary loss in order to render greater service or tide the public over a crisis? It cannot be done. It is profit first, and then, perhaps, as much service as is compatible with profit.

Now this primary and essential preoccupation with making

a profit naturally tends to color a business man's view of his entire world, and is what, in my opinion, mainly differentiates business from the professions. Nor do I speak as an impractical intellectual. Of the last thirty years I have spent about one-half in business and half in professional work, and I realize the great difference, having paid my monthly bills, between concentrating primarily on the work rather than the profit.

Moreover, dealing inevitably with material things and with the satisfying of the world's material wants, the business man tends to locate happiness in *them* rather than in the intellectual and spiritual unless he constantly refreshes his spirit away from business during his leisure. When the pressure of business on his time, or his concentration on it, becomes so great as to preclude his reasonable use of leisure for the development of his whole human personality, he is apt to become a complete materialist even if, as is now frequently not the case, he ever had it in him to become anything else. He may live in a palace, ride in the most luxurious cars and fill his rooms with old masters and the costliest manuscripts which his wealth can draw from under the hammer at Christie's but if he cares more for riches, luxury, and power than for a humanely rounded life he is not civilized but what the Greeks properly called a "barbarian."

Aside from narrowness of interests, the business man, from the nature of his major occupation, is apt to have short views and to distrust all others. It was once said, as superlative praise, of the late J. P. Morgan, one of the most public spirited and far-sighted business men we have had, that he "thought in ten-year periods." Most business men think—

[19]

and do well to do so as business men—in one or two-year periods; the business man cares nothing for the tendency of what he is doing. This has been emphasized in the American business man by the vast extent of the natural resources with which he has had to deal and the recuperative powers of an active people in a half-settled continent. If, as he did in the northern Mississippi Valley, he can make his personal profit by ripping the forests off the face of half a dozen states in a decade, he is content to let those who come later look after themselves.

Nor is he any more solicitous about the social results of his activities. Obviously, what interests the business man as a business man is a free hand to gather wealth as quickly as may be, combined with a guarantee that society shall protect him in that wealth once he has gathered it. He may steal the water resources of a dozen states but, once they are stolen, he is a defender of the Constitution and the sanctity of contract. It is not hard to understand why the United States is the most radical country in the world in its business methods and the most conservative in its political!

Preoccupation with profit, again, tends to make a business man, as business man, blind to the æsthetic quality in life. A beautiful bit of scenery, such as Montauk Point, is for him merely a good site for a real-estate development; a waterfall is merely water power. America's most successful business man, Mr. Ford, while rolling up millions by the hundreds in profits, was content to turn out what was, perhaps, the ugliest car on the market. It was only when his profits were threatened that he turned to the consideration of beauty, and he would not have done so had it not promised profit. No sane business man in charge of a large

[20]

business would do so. It is much the same with the cultivation of the business man's mind. Time is money, and anything which takes time and does not give business results is waste. But if you tell him that if he shows an interest in Keats he can probably land Smith's account—Smith being a queer, moony guy—or that if he will go to hear the "Rheingold" he can make a hit with that chap he has long been after, the effect will be magical. Innumerable advertisements of books or teaching of foreign languages will easily illustrate what I mean.

These and other qualities of the business man are his qualities *as* a business man. They are qualities that are bred in him by his occupation. Plenty of business men are much more than business men and outside of their offices and business hours have other qualities and other interests. But there is this to be said. Society at large, including the business man himself, owes its opportunity for a fully rounded life mainly to those who have not been business men. What will be the effect on all of us of the growing dominance of the business type and of the hold which the business man and business ideals have attained upon our civilization?

III

Before we discuss this let me gladly admit that the business man's search for a profit has in many ways been of great cultural, as well as material, benefit to the community at large. I am by no means decrying business. If the business man has not, culturally, been a creator, he has done marvellous work as a middleman. In the phonograph and the radio, for example, the business man has brought the work of the scientist on the one hand and the musician on the other together in such a way that the lonely resident of a country village can listen to the symphony orchestra of perhaps a half-dozen cities. The business man, indeed, does not care a rap whether Jones listens to a symphony or a prize fight, but he has given him an opportunity. Yet that opportunity could not come to Jones unless both the abstract scientist, reaching the business man through the medium of the inventor, and the musical composer had existed and done their work in a spirit quite remote from business. In a world entirely made up of business men (with the qualities of business men only) it is doubtful if either pure science or music would have existed.

Taking this cultural aspect of a possible business man's civilization worked out to its final result, we may note several things. If modern business is not a profession—and I certainly do not believe it is—it, nevertheless, has become an intensely absorbing occupation. Moreover, like science and most of modern life, it has become highly specialized, both for workmen and for executives. At no time before in the history of the world have the occupations of all men tended to render them so lopsided. Never before have leisure and a wise use of it been so necessary. The functions of the lawyer and doctor, even of the thinker and the artist, have become narrowed to only a small part of the field formerly covered by them. Compare for example a modern scientist in any branch with a Bacon, or a modern painter with men like Michelangelo or da Vinci,—easel painters, mural decorators, poets, architects, sculptors, military engineers, and other things by turns. The narrowing of the field of work for all men has greatly intensified the need of their finding opportunity for the development of other sides of their personalities in pursuits other than their major ones. This is most true of the business man because of the effect upon him of his work as contrasted with the professions and other careers. The danger lurks in exactly that situation; for the one who most needs, but least realizes, the value of leisure and culture, of a fully rounded personality, of what we may call humanism, is the one who has become the controller of the destinies of all.

In the remainder of this article we can but glance briefly at some of the effects, already becoming visible, of the dominance of business ideals. Let us take first the question of that leisure so essential from the standpoint of a humane civilization. In an economic civilization in which efficiency is the one great good, leisure will be considered as waste save in so far as it promotes the individual's productive capacity in his next stint of work. Having little use for sanely occupied leisure themselves, our business spokesmen try either to confuse it in the public mind with idleness or to make people utilize it for the satisfaction of more material wants. Thus in his *American Omen*, which we may take as an ultra-expression of the new business ideal, Garrett says, speaking of leisure, that the American "does not know what to do with idleness. He does not understand it. Generally it kills him." Again, speaking of adult education, he adds that "in England the intent of adult education is to give the wage earner a cultural interest to fill up his leisure time— nature study, astronomy, the physics and chemistry of everyday life, literature, perhaps. In Germany the intent is technical. In Denmark it is to stimulate the mind generally. In France there is not much of any kind. But," he adds triumphantly, "the American idea of adult education is to enable a man to find greater self-expression in his job." Certainly from the standpoint of humanism, of a fully rounded human existence, no comment on this business ideal is needed.

If it be claimed that Garrett does not speak responsibly for business, let us turn to another spokesman. Harvard University has taken the lead in giving its scholastic benediction to business, which it proclaims in stone over the entrance to its Business School, given to it by one of the richest business men in America, to be "the oldest of the arts, the newest of the professions." Doctor Carver, professor of economics at Harvard, writes that in America "we may take a certain genuine satisfaction in the fact that we have no leisure class and are never likely to have one . . . though we do fall behind in those arts that are commonly cultivated by a leisure class . . . and must therefore content ourselves with such arts and graces as can be cultivated by busy people."

It is obvious, except to our "practical" business men, that there are many kinds of work, not only like the arts, needful for humanism, but like pure science, needful for business itself, that can be the fruit only of free time and of the absence of the need to turn the results into immediate cash. Yet here again we run counter to the new business ideals as promulgated by Professor Carver. "Generally with some exceptions," he writes, "the more useful the person the more he is paid," adding that "if a pupil shows a special aptitude for a kind of work which is being overdone and poorly paid, to train the pupil for that work would be to condemn him to poverty, and no conscientious educator would care to do that. He must, in fact, train the pupil for a kind of work which is reasonably well paid." We need not add the recent dictum of another professor that the best standard of value of a piece of literary work is, after all, what it will fetch in the market, to see how the new leaven of the business ideals of profits and "service" are working in our academic minds. "The greater the service rendered, the greater is the personal income" (we may thus syllogize this idea), "therefore, we can estimate the service in terms of income, and (with no selfish philosophy, of course, only idealism) we must train our boys to make the largest incomes possible so that they may be sure they are rendering the greatest service to society." Q.E.D. Naturally the business men, whose badge of success is income, applaud such a theory, for it establishes indubitably that the owner of a cigar-store chain is infinitely more valuable to humanity than a Keats, even though from every past civilization the only things which remain of value to humanity are the creative works of those who were not business men. The business men of those days are as forgotten and indistinguishable as the leaves of yesteryears in Vallombrosa. Nothing could bring out more clearly than this barbarous syllogism and philosophy the difference between a humanistic and an economic civilization.

We may also note the changes occurring in the spirit of the professions as they conform themselves to the dominant note of a business man's civilization. That civilization, as we have said, cloaks its crudity under the name of service, yet even in the medical profession, perhaps as yet the least tainted, what is the service rendered as compared with a generation ago? Many articles in our magazines have dealt with the seriousness of the crisis which is overtaking whole

[25]

countrysides where no physican can now be found to labor for little pay, and the difficulties of finding medical service even in the cities at low cost or at moments inconvenient for the doctor, such as night calls. But if social service can be calculated in income, why not? If the theory is true, is it not a doctor's duty to leave a whole countryside to struggle without medical care if it can pay him only three or four thousand a year when in a city he can make twenty thousand if he gets in with the right people?

The same applies even more to the legal profession. The great prizes in this are for the most part now to be won only from the great business men and their corporations. A man may struggle in private practice for twenty years and not make in all that time what a more fortunate fellow may get as a retainer from a railroad or a water-power trust in one year. The business-civilization ideal of wealth as distinction would be a powerful influence tending to make the lawyer turn to business in any case, but now the new business philosophy of service measured by income makes that turning a social duty and salves the professional conscience.

Another profession, architecture, is beginning to feel the influence of the dominance of business. We have good architects in America—none better—but business does not give them their chance. Buildings are built to sell, and, being built on borrowed money on speculation, must be sold as quickly as possible. No chances can be taken on not pleasing the taste of the public. Moreover, in buildings every inch of space must be made to bring in rent. In every direction the architect's hands are tied. In many cases, partly from

[26]

the spread of the business ideal of life and partly perhaps from despair, the architect has come to adopt the attitude expressed by one of the well-known ones recently. "As an architect," he writes, "I am really just a manufacturer of a commodity known as building space, and my job, as I see it, is to make as attractive a package as is physically or æsthetically possible for me in view of all the conditions imposed." The consequence is that in architectural experiment America is falling so rapidly behind countries like Denmark, Holland, Germany, Austria, and even Russia, that after studying the new buildings, particularly the private houses in those countries, returning to America is almost like going back to the early Victorian age. I have not been to Russia, but the noted French architect Le Corbusier has recently gone there to investigate the new buildings and he reports of the Muscovites that "their works are a splendid outburst of lyrical poetry. They are poets in steel and glass." The picture of the new "Palace of Industry" at Charkov certainly goes far to confirm this opinion. Much of the new architecture I have seen and the marvellously interesting new bloom everywhere in the countries which I have named makes the American revamping of the English, Colonial, and Spanish types seem to belong to a past world. Plagiarism is a confession of sterility. Of all the new movement and the new method of living it entails, the American public is almost totally ignorant. The business man with an eye solely to an immediate profit, and the architect who considers himself a business man, "just a manufacturer of a commodity known as building space," are not likely to carry America far on any new road.

[27]

IV

Of the effect of a business man's civilization on the manners of society I shall speak in a later chapter and need not here anticipate what I shall there say. We may note, however, in passing, its effect on taste and habits. As for taste, a business civilization has as its core the idea of a money profit and of a material standard of values. Business men devote their tireless energy to creating new wants which their factories can supply. But two points must be noticed. One is that these wants which they create and foster must be material or there is no manufacturing to supply them and no profit to the business man. If people wish to tramp about the countryside remote from motor cars, or read a book or go to an art museum or simply engage in intelligent conversation at home, the manufacturer is losing a possible profit. The constant endeavor of modern business is therefore to get people to fill up their leisure with *things*, things that can be made and sold. Another point with regard even to these things is, that the great profits being in mass-production, the wants so scientifically created by advertising are such as may be made to appeal to the masses. The spiritual or æsthetic value of the new wants is bound to be made subordinate to the possibility of their being filled in quantity.

Some of the problems touched upon, as well as others, are world problems. Their special importance in America is due to the curiously lopsided development which American civilization has increasingly followed. With the unique position that the business man has here attained to impress himself upon the entire cultural life of the people, the dangers of certain business tendencies are enormously increased as compared with other countries where the ideals and activities of the business man meet with checks from many other influences, contemporary or historic, in the civilization as a whole. Even if the American business man were alive to the enormous social responsibility of the position in which he finds himself, it is not likely that he could assume the rôles in civilization which have hitherto been taken by a dozen or so classes of other types, that he could include within himself all the springs to thought and action and all the checks and balances which a variety of social types have hitherto supplied. For one thing, the prime factor in business life, the need for making a profit, is at war with the spirit of all the arts and with what should be the spirit of the professions. Again, the training in taking short views, the ignoring of the future results of action beyond a reasonable period of profit, the subordinating to the thought of profit of all the larger social implications of action, are among the characteristics of business as business that do not augur well for placing the supreme control of the entire national civilization in business hands. The business man, moreover, is merely a purveyor and not a creator of the real values of a civilization. If under his dominance the business philosophy indicated above takes—as it seems to be doing—increasing hold upon the universities, the churches, the professions, and the people at large, it may be asked how long shall we have any creators?

If the fundamental idea underlying our civilization, its *primum mobile*, is to become that of a business profit, it is inevitable that we shall decline in the scale of what has hitherto been considered civilization as contrasted with barbarism in the Greek sense. The Harvard professor may dismiss lightly the loss of the "arts and graces," but if his doctrine of the valuation of social service in terms of income is to become established, is it not much more likely to be lost than the "arts and graces"? What becomes of the artistic spirit, of the professional spirit, of the pure scientific spirit? The American is apt to think of his own country as in the van of at least everything material and of Europe as negligible; but even in the things considered distinctly American we are falling behind. That we have recently lost the speed record both on land and water with that special darling of America, the gasoline engine, may not be important, but it will surprise most Americans to know that both the fastest and the average speed of all trains in England and some parts of the Continent are higher than in America. In aerial passenger routes America, in spite of the efforts to make it appear otherwise, is far behind Europe, where the whole continent is covered with a network of aerial routes used as readily as we use trains at home.

I have touched at some length on architecture because it was not many years ago that we were hoping for a genuine renaissance that should have its beginning in America, and because we have, as I said, some absolutely first-class architects. The present renaissance, however, has come wholly in Europe from men like Le Corbusier in France, Gropius in Germany, or Oud in Holland, with their enthusiastic followers. We have had so little to do with it and are sharing so little in it that the most recent pronouncement on the new movement there dismisses the United States in three lines as offering nothing of theoretical value.

Civilizations rest fundamentally upon ideas. These ideas to be effective must be those of the dominant classes in the civilization. In making the business men the dominant and sole class in America, that country is making the experiment of resting her civilization on the ideas of business men. The other classes, dominated by the business one, are rapidly conforming in their philosophy of life to it. The business man, in so far as he is more than a business type, in so far as he is a fully rounded personality (as, I repeat, many of them now are), owes that development of himself outside his work to the work of other classes in the past or present. If those classes become merged in his own, whither can even he himself look for his extra-occupational development? If the leaders are not humanely rounded personalities, civilized rather than barbarian, what shall be expected of the mass which patterns itself upon them? In a word, can a great civilization be built up or maintained upon the philosophy of the counting-house and the sole basic idea of a profit?

CHAPTER II
THE COST OF
PROSPERITY

THE COST OF PROSPERITY

I

Not long ago a despatch from Washington announced that "the highest standard of living ever attained in the history of the world was reached last year [1926] by the American people," and gave as basis for the statement the government's figure for the income of our population, which income was set at ninety billion dollars. The "high standard" thus indicated is unhesitatingly accepted by almost everyone; but even if we do accept as a fact, though it is far from being a universal one, the ability of all persons to spend more and to buy more things than ever before, it may be worth while to consider what some of the by-products of the processes involved have been. Overwhelmed by the material advance made in the past five decades or so and by the vast amount of Pollyanna literature with which we are flooded by politicians and business executives with axes to grind, we are apt to lose sight of the law of compensation and to think of all change as unalloyed improvement.

Change may or may not be "progress," but whether it is or not it is bound to involve compensatory losses. Man may have advanced far from his ancestor which lived in the primeval slime, but that lowly progenitor could breathe either in air or water and if he lost a leg could grow another. To-day man can make his voice heard three thousand miles away, but he dies if you hold his nose in a water basin and is a cripple for life when he loses a foot. What he gains in one direction he drops in another, unpopular as Nature or anyone else may be when they tell him so. One is not necessarily a pessimist, therefore, when one chooses to consider what losses may have been entailed by attaining to the present "highest standard of living."

Two points are notable in the popular belief as to that standard. One is that all classes in the community are supposed somehow to share in its beneficences, and the other is that the measuring rod used is material and economic. The leaders in the "marvellous advance" are automobiles, radios, vacuum cleaners, electric washing machines, telephones, etc. It is assumed that spiritual and intellectual progress will somehow come also from the mere accumulation of "things," and this assumption has become a sort of American religion with all the psychological implications of religious dogma. In business circles, mass-production, on which our present prosperity is based, is not considered merely as a transient and possibly an unsound economic phase, but as the creator of "the highest standard of living ever attained," and, as such, as little to be doubted or questioned as God the Creator before Darwin. At any rate, mass-production is so closely linked to the ninety billion dollars that the two may be considered as the heads and tails of the same coin, and the by-products of one those of the other.

It may be noted that, although ninety billion dollars is a staggering sum to contemplate, we receive something of a shock when we read farther that the average income of all persons "gainfully employed" was $2210 a year. When we turn to another statistical source and find that nearly ten thousand persons paid taxes on incomes of from $100,000 to

[36]

$1,000,000 year each, two hundred and twenty-eight on incomes over $1,000,000, and fourteen on incomes of over $5,000,000 each, we begin to wonder whether the masses are getting quite their share of the benefits of mass-production. It is evident that however great the "national" wealth may be, there is something very queer about its distribution, and that the gulf between the average man and the rich man has widened with appalling rapidity.

We are not here concerned primarily with that point nor with the average person "gainfully employed," whose income is evidently not much above $2000, but we may glance a moment at the condition of the latter in order to get some standard of income measurement. In 1917 the street railway employees in Seattle submitted a minimum budget for living in a dispute with their company over wages. They figured that $1917.88 annually for a family of five would allow, among other things, $12 for the education of the children, $30 for reading matter of all kinds, and $120 each for insurance and old-age savings. The company was able to reduce this to $1505.60 by eliminating all reading matter, including newspapers, reducing education from $12 to $11, old-age savings from $120 to $100, and insurance from $120 to $30. Carfare was reduced to $35.70 annually, with the somewhat ironical result that the members of the families of the men engaged in running the street cars were allowed only enough to use a car themselves on an average of once every six days! As $5 a year per person was allowed for "recreation" and $4 for all "miscellaneous," we need not linger over the average man in our total population who is "gainfully employed" when considering for the moment the high standard of living. We are here concerned with the persons

[37]

between those and the ultra wealthy—the persons who both suffer from and enjoy factors in that standard.

One of the outstanding features of life to-day is its frightful and steadily increasing cost. Apart from taxation, it is much higher in the United States than in any of the other ten countries in which I have spent longer or shorter periods in the past few years. This is in part due to the intentionally prohibitive tariff, in part to the terrific increase in wages, and in part to the increase in the kind and number of things we are supposed to have in order to be happy.

Those who defend the present wage schedules are forever telling us that they do not increase the cost of living because of the increased output per man and the increased savings in cost due to new machinery and mass-production. Much of this, of course, is sheer bunkum. For the housekeeper who pays a cook anywhere from $75 to $100 as compared with $25 to $30 fifteen years ago there is a clear loss in the family budget with no increased output whatever. The cook gets the full benefit of all the labor-saving devices, and the mistress pays for these and the advanced wages as well. When the other day I had some bookshelves put up and paid two of the stupidest workmen it has ever been my luck to encounter $12 a day each there was no compensating advantage whatever. I am told I might have got it done for less had I taken the trouble to find a "scab" workman out of work. In the first place I do not know where to find one and in the second place it would not have been necessary fifteen years ago. I could then have gone to any union shop and had the job done reasonably. No, a factory may increase wages and lower costs, but the ordinary householder cannot do so in all that

[38]

affects the running of his home and family. The increase of wages, in many cases to prohibitive levels, is the heaviest single burden, except rent, to the man of moderate means to-day.

But to a great extent the increase in living cost is due also to the increase in the number of things. We live so fast and heedlessly that we seldom consider how much of our present annual expense is made up of costs incurred for things that few of us used fifteen or twenty years ago. Of course the automobile bulks largest in this respect as a single item. In the well-to-do New York suburb where I lived for some years before the War, comparatively few people had cars. Most of the commuters of the class then spending $8000 to $10,000 a year—the equivalent of $15,000 to $20,000 to-day —always walked to and from the station, taking a hack in bad weather. To day there are over twenty million cars in the country, or about one to every family. If one examines the real-estate advertisements one finds that now a small modern house will have its vacuum cleaner, its washing machine, elaborate wiring with outlets all over the place, its cedar closets, electric refrigerator, radio, automatic heat-regulator, its several bathrooms, and a garage for one, and not seldom two cars, to mention some of what are considered essentials. I do not question the comfort and convenience of at least most of these things, but their steady multiplication adds heavily to the burden of the man who has to pay for them in order to maintain his family according to the "American standard." For all with incomes of from $5000 to $50,000 the burden is almost equally felt, for standards of expense are in proportion to income and annually mounting.

[39]

II

The demand for luxury even in the transaction of ordinary business is adding tremendously to the overhead expense of doing it and so to the cost of goods or services. A railway station must be as magnificent as a Roman bath. Our shops must be housed in Renaissance palaces on expensive streets. We are told that expensive office furniture is the safest investment in the world. A "front," whether of clothes, furnishing, building, or location, must always be put up so as to indicate wealth back of it all or the business may not be considered sound, profitable, and "up-to-date." Salesmanship has become increasingly expensive. I was recently talking with a woman who has an excellent salary (forming, of course, part of the overhead of her department), in one of the supposedly less extravagant shops. She complained of the expense she was under because of the high standard of salesmanship demanded by her customers. Fifteen years ago, she said, if she had dared to appear in the costly clothes the house now *makes* her wear, she would have been promptly discharged. She has to go to the theaters, know the latest plays and books, and be able to chat with her customers, not about her goods, but socially by the half-hour. Her sales are splendid—with prices according.

Fifteen years ago almost every physician, dentist, or oculist had his office in a room in his own home and rarely had an assistant. Now almost without exception they have to take an office in some apartment house at rents of from $1200 to $3000 a year, and employ at least one uniformed nurse in attendance—expenses which, of course, are borne by the patients. To a considerable extent this is the fault of the

[40]

patients themselves. There is an instinctive tendency to feel if a doctor still has his office in his home with only a maid to answer the bell that he is either not up-to-date in knowledge or is unsuccessful for some reason. I know of one very able medical man who has deliberately done so and who has tried to keep down his professional expense for the benefit of his patients, but several of these patients have more than hinted to him that they would prefer to have a more expensive car standing at their door when he makes his call!

To an incredible degree we have most of us unthinkingly adopted the cost standard as the value standard. Some time ago a prosperous and practical inventor disclosed some of his adventures with popular psychology. He had invented a small article which, with fair sales, could make a large profit when retailed at ten cents. He sent out a number of street hawkers to sell the article, half of them with the thing priced at ten cents and the other half with a twenty-five-cent price. The latter sold immediately whereas few were sold at the lower price.

Often the influence of this false standard is more insidious and disastrous. I was discussing the matter the other day with an internationally known scientist. He was at one time—but is no longer—a professor in one of our leading universities. He said that when his first child was born he was getting a salary of $2500 a year. The leading obstetrician in the town charged $500 for a "baby case"—one-fifth of my friend's annual income. When the financial situation was explained the doctor told him that his assistant was just as able a medical man as himself and would charge only $100, and that he himself would be on the telephone ready to come in a moment if anything went wrong. My friend, after wrestling in his mind for some time, decided to have the assistant, but he told me that he hoped never again to go through such hell as he endured during the hours of birth, when he thought that if anything went wrong with his wife he would feel all his life that he had sacrificed her for the four hundred dollars' difference. Yet I consider that this man has the sanest and most balanced mind of all the men I know.

The situation outlined is a very real and, both financially and psychologically, a serious one. When anyone we love is ill we feel impelled to have the best attention for him, a half-dozen specialists if necessary; and the standard of the best, more subtly than we realize, is the cost standard. We have become hypersensitive, and this sensitiveness is terrifically costly. I myself was born in New York of a well-to-do family. My mother's father was rich as things then went. Yet it could not have cost at most $100 to bring me into the world. There were no graduate nurses, no maternity hospitals, few, if any, specialists. The ordinary family physician, at $2 a house visit, and two women such as we call practical nurses did everything, in the home. To-day, what with doctors, nurses, and the hospital charge, the cost would run to about $1500 for a family of the same social grade, or fifteen times the old cost, whereas the ordinary income has less than trebled.

III

The increased cost of living from these and other causes is having marked effects. It is, for one thing, largely destroying the old idea of thrift and saving in the classes with which we are here concerned. In the first place, there is the natural human desire to possess many of the new things available for their own sakes, and often because Mrs. Jones has them, and they belong to the new standard. But there are more insidious forces at work. Mass-production requires an enormous and steady output to be profitable. There is a saturation point for nearly every article. Fresh vegetables are eaten up in a day or two, but clothes or cars may last several years. There is no reason why many of the mechanical contrivances we buy should not in themselves last many years. From the standpoint of the producer there is always the danger that the consumer may have enough of any particular article unless he is made to want more. This is accomplished in several ways in the technic which has been developed by psychologically trained sales experts. The consumer is cleverly induced to want an article that he had thought he could do without or could not afford. If he has already owned one, as an automobile, the slogan becomes that every self-respecting family should have two. The model is changed every year and social vanity is played upon; or an appeal is made to the powerful motives of fear, shame, and pride. In selling many of the mechanical contrivances a more brutal method is employed. Manufacturers stop making essential parts so as to require the owner to buy an entirely new and perhaps only slightly altered model. Some years ago, for instance, I bought at a cost of $450 a certain instrument. It was good for a lifetime. I added steadily, as I could afford it, to the things that were to be used with it, and without which it was useless, until the whole investment was over $800. One day when I went to get more, I was told they no longer made anything for that "model," I would have to get another and, of course, with a condescending tone that was almost a sneer, "I must want to have the latest." The new model, differing only slightly from the old, cost, the salesman told me, as though it were a trifle, $750. To accumulate the same things to go with it that I had for the old would cost about $400 more. My old investment was rendered worthless, and the salesman made it evident that he had no interest in a person so cheap that he would not casually throw away $800 and spend $1,000 more on a toy. His company did not have the least glimmer of an idea of responsibility toward a public out of which it had made its money and which had made, in the aggregate, a colossal investment in its instruments. When other methods fail and you really have no money, the advantages of the partial payment plan are glowingly placed before you.

Again, we are told by leaders of the world of mass-production that thrift is out of date. One of the greatest manufacturers in the country recently wrote that "use" not "saving" should govern our ideas with respect to our national and other resources. In another remarkable pronouncement, this man, who is an idol of a large part of the people, said that no boy had ever succeeded or would succeed who saved money when he was young. Another leader writes that "one reason for America's prosperity and one reason, in my opinion, why that prosperity will continue, is that we have committed ourselves to a standard of living far beyond our wildest pre-war dreams. . . . We cannot make good except by producing more wealth, and always a little ahead of us is advertising with its alluring images of still other good things that work will buy. Americans have passed out of the period where they care about petty economies. They want convenience. They want

[44]

action. They want comfort and style. It is impossible to call Americans back to petty thrift, and I personally am glad of it. . . . I live now in New York where everybody expects to be overcharged and where nobody counts the dimes, much less the pennies. . . . We have ceased to count our pennies in America, and I certainly hope we never return to the days of the most graceless of all virtues, a niggardly and penny-pinching thrift."

One wonders just what spiritual joy there should be in being overcharged. Also, most of us have still to count the dimes. The other day I wanted a mere bite of luncheon in a hurry. Going into the only business men's restaurant in sight, I paid one dime to have my hat checked, another to the boy who insisted on handing me a towel in the washroom, and another for the cover charge; and I wondered what, over the old days, was the advantage in paying at the rate of a hundred hard-earned dollars a year for an ordinary snack of lunch without getting anything to eat.

There are other factors at work to make thrift appear hopeless and so to destroy the average man's peace of mind as he contemplates old age or possible long incapacity from illness. One is the fact that savings do not seem to go anywhere when made from a modest income. Although the cost of living has easily tripled in thirty years, the income from most sound investments has not gone up at all. When one saves a thousand dollars and contemplates the $50 or even $60 a year that that will bring in income, and thinks how many fifties or sixties it will take to support him and his family, he wonders whether it is worth while to pinch for so meager a result. Moreover, owing to advancing costs and the changing scale of living, there is no telling what the cost of living may be not merely in one's old age but even ten years hence.

Before the pace of living started on its now annually accelerated speed, a man could forecast with reasonable certainty what income would enable him to maintain his relative position in his stratum of society for the fifteen or twenty years of life that might be left to him when he retired. Now, apart from other factors, an invention one year means a luxury on the market in another two or three, and that luxury becomes a necessity, like the automobile, in another three or four. In a recent study of the income and expenses of nearly a hundred families of the members of the faculty of the University of California it is shown that the average savings per family including life insurance are $360. The annual cost of medical service alone among them is $325. A New York professional man who considered this article, when read to him, unduly pessimistic, admitted that although he lives on a scale indicated by his rent of $2500 a year he is unable to save anything. The surprising extent to which the hope and even the thought of providing for old age has gone from the mind of the moderately well-to-do was still further shown by this man's comment that life insurance was the equivalent of savings. Life insurance is excellent and essential, but only in its more expensive forms does it permit the insurer himself to enjoy the benefits of it, and straight life policies are not complete protection for one's own old age. Even if one insures against accident, sickness, and death, there are many emergencies in life which can be met only from one's own saved money. Is it any wonder that there has been a rush in the last decade for common stocks and speculation when the newspapers continually tell of stupendous profits (and advance in "values" of nearly two and a half billions in one month alone), when business leaders decry thrift, and the cost of living gives us a kick from behind? Even the President of the United States and the Secretary of the Treasury encourage the people to speculate, and in the *New York Times* I read that the Mellon family made $300,000,000 in a year. I know many men who have large salaries and many who have accumulated fortunes but I do not know a single one who has accumulated more than the merest competency except from gift, inheritance, or advances in stocks. For some years the stock market may have been an ever-present help in time of need to many, but stocks cannot continue to the end of our lives to climb an endless escalator; and as one looks forward to an eternal making of money to buy an endless succession of new things, or even merely of new "models," one wonders whether the "highest standard ever attained" is really worth all it costs and whether if Wordsworth could to-day see the richest nation in the world he would not be more than ever convinced that "Getting and spending, we lay waste our powers." Yet still the high-powered sales forces urge "buy, buy, buy and make yourselves and everybody prosperous by it." We are hearing a good deal about prosperity without profit. We may soon be giving consideration to prosperity without peace of mind. It is a fact not without its significance, perhaps, for social trends and tendencies that when the disaster in Florida and Porto Rico occurred a year ago, less than one person in a thousand in the richest city in our country, a country formerly quick to respond to the call for help, has contributed even one of those dimes we are told are so unconsidered in New York.

[47]

IV

Let us turn to some of the other social effects of this high standard. It is obvious that with a national income of even ninety billions, a hundred and twenty million people cannot buy everything. Some things have to go if we are to have new things constantly and pay double or treble for the old. We are electing, in many cases perforce, to let go the home. This is due partly to the cost of housing and partly to that of servants as well as general costs. In the urban centers, at least, gild the pill as we may, the people who fifteen years ago had comfortable homes are by no means so comfortable to-day. The New York papers advertise "beautiful one-room homes" consisting of a room eleven by fourteen with a bath, a bed that folds up into the wall, and a cooking shelf in a dark closet. The one I have in mind costs as much in yearly rent as twenty-five years ago the dignified three-story eleven-room house on one of the finest streets in town cost my father—that is, $1200. Even if one succeeds in finding a five- to seven-room apartment, with one or two of the rooms of good size, at $2000 (which is by no means easy to do), one has only half the space at about double the cost of two decades back, and nothing like the dignity, quiet, or privacy. Moreover, the maid service, when it can be afforded, is at two to three times the former cost.

In the pre-war days a good neighborhood was usually sufficiently large to permit of extensive walks in it. To-day in New York even a very expensive neighborhood is as frequently as not an oasis of a block or two, or even an apartment house or two, in the midst of a desert of dreary and depressing slums. The rookery quarters of a medieval city may be picturesque. The slums of New York are merely drab and sordid. To those accustomed to a house or even to the spaciousness of a better-class Paris apartment the usual New York apartment seems hopelessly cramped and lacking in all character and dignity. The rooms seem almost to open into one another and the family to be always on top of one another, whether taking their baths or entertaining guests. And guests are infinitely more of a problem than they ever were. Overnight guests are out of the question for most people of moderate means. It is hard enough to get an apartment which affords decent living for the family, not to speak of a guest room. The lack of service, the dependence upon one maid, when any, instead of upon the invariable cook and waitress of even the modest families of twenty years back, has made entertaining a genuine and not seldom an insoluble problem for families living on such incomes as before the War would have made hospitality merely an easy and gracious function of household life.

Moreover, within the family itself, the close quarters of the modern apartment afford infinitely more opportunity for friction of tempers and temperaments than the old homes. A third-story front bedroom as an escape from the family sitting-room two stories below had almost the aloofness of a mountain peak. The unsatisfactory character of the new homes, or the unsatisfied natures of their tenants, are proved beyond dispute by the restlessness engendered. Last October (1928) in New York alone a hundred thousand families, involving at the lowest estimate three hundred thousand people, moved from one apartment to another. What memories can cluster about his "childhood home" for a child who is thus annually dragged from one set of rooms to another by parents in search of cheaper rents or the latest installations in the way of electric iceboxes or garbage incinerators? Perhaps sunshine, air, quiet, spaciousness, decency of neighborhood, dignity, privacy are aristocratic requirements, vestiges of a now lost mode of comely and gracious living. At any rate, they are now the most expensiye "things" to acquire, when they can be acquired at all, in a great modern city. Yet two decades ago even in New York and Brooklyn they were readily obtainable on such modest incomes as $3000 or $4000 a year.

V

What has been the effect on the professional and intellectual classes? Of course where they have linked themselves to big business or made their work fit into mass-production they have weathered the storm of the high standard very well. No one need worry about the general counsel of a motor-car company, the artists who draw the syndicated comic strips, or the movie stars. But there are whole classes who do not or cannot thus fit in. A nationally known trust company officer recently wrote that most of those who disliked the present situation and who were given to dire comment or prophecy were merely those who had had comfortable incomes before the present high standard hit us and who had been unable to adjust themselves to it, that is, make *large* incomes. But according to the present modes of dividing the national income, how *can* these classes thus adjust themselves except by abandoning their work and going into business?

Our glance at the minimum wage budget prepared by

the street railway men has shown us what can be done on $1900 a year: $12 a year for education, $30 for all reading matter (one-third of which would be consumed by one daily paper), and $12.20 for tobacco and all recreation. The average pay of all clergymen throughout the United States is $735 a year. Even if this frequently includes a house, how are they to adjust themselves? To attain even to the minimum budget of the street railway worker they would nearly have to more than double their income, that is, to give approximately one-third of their time to the work of their ministry and two-thirds to making money solely. Even if they could do so, what would they get as their share of the "high standard"? We have seen that even the street railway company had to cut out all reading matter, even newspapers, from the homes of its men if they were to live on $1505. Yet under the high standard the country allows its clergy scarcely half that sum and complains that the church is failing in leadership.

Let us turn to another class, which is great numerically and should be great in influence, and which we shall consider more particularly in a later chapter. The average pay of teachers throughout the country districts of the Middle Atlantic States, including that manufactory of millionaires, Pennsylvania, is $870 a year; in the villages it is $1244. Let us bear in mind the bleak budget of $1900 of the street railway men and remember also that the conductor of a railway freight train gets about $3750 a year and the engineer about $4700. What are the opportunities and prospects for a man of scholarly tastes, attainments, and pursuits? The average pay of over eleven thousand members of college faculties is less than $3000 a year, and, although in rare institutions a comparatively few men may attain to $8000 or $10,000, a man is fortunate indeed who gets from $5000 to $7000. How are these men to adjust themselves? Most of them do do extra work to earn money as, in forty per cent of the cases, do the wives also. In the days before the "high standard" a vacation was a vacation, a period in which the professor, fagged from nine months' drilling of immature minds, could rest and catch up on his professional reading, get fresh points of view and prepare for the next nine months' bout with inquiring or resisting youth. Now, we read, one-third of the faculty could take no vacation at all; 40 per cent took less than two weeks, and 60 per cent less than four weeks; yet yesterday the men in the building trades in New York laid down their demand for every Saturday off on full pay, equivalent to six and a half weeks' vacation from purely physical work requiring practically no mental preparation or recuperation. Is it any wonder that a professor at Berkeley on $3000 a year goes into business at $20,000 a year, that a professor from an Eastern university on about $6000 a year becomes president of a business company with $75,000 a year drawing account, and that another turns from teaching history to writing advertisements, to mention the three who occur first to me?

Let us glance at writing under the high standard. Big incomes can be earned by anything adapted for mass-production, such as best-selling novels (with possible movie rights), articles for the mass-circulation magazines, certain sorts of "syndicated stuff," and so on; but that sort of writing is not the most valuable for our national culture as a rule. The cost of living is certainly from 200 to 250 per cent of what it was in the decade before the War. "Index figures" are misleading. It is of little importance to the average man whether pig lead is up 25 or 50 per cent. It is of prime importance to him that, as I can show by my checkbook, a cook who cost $30 a month then costs $75 now, that a suit of clothes which cost $28 then costs at the same store $74 now, and so on; to say nothing of all the new things to be bought. Of course, the changes in wage schedules would differ from newspaper to newspaper, but in one which gave me the figures for before the War and now I find that editorial salaries have advanced 50 per cent, junior reporters and book reviewers the same, poets 25 per cent, whereas, rather oddly, space writers get actually 10 per cent less than before. I am told that writers for the high-grade magazines get about double. Comparing the flat price paid for scholarly volumes in two similar works twenty years ago and now, I found that the scholars working to-day were paid no more than before the War. On a royalty basis, owing to higher book prices and larger sales, authors probably fare better than fifteen years ago, though strict comparison for many reasons is difficult. On the whole, taking the ordinary man of letters who lives by his output and who writes books, articles, reviews, and does the other various literary jobs, it would seem that in order to maintain himself in the same relative position in the social and economic scale he would have to increase his output very materially.

Business rewards are greater than ever for those who are successful, but granted the social value of the business man's services and granted also the "dignity of labor," it may well be asked whether a standard of living is really intrinsically high which thus places additional burdens on the shoulders of whole classes of the country's spiritual and intellectual

[53]

leadership, its clergymen, its teachers, and writers, in order to lighten the load of the carpenters, cooks, and chambermaids. It may be truly said that Society has always expected the intellectual classes to content themselves to a great extent with rewards that are not pecuniary. That is so, but the tremendous advance in the standard of living and the tremendously increased gulf between the man of large income and the man of a moderate one has served to depress these classes in the comparative scale far below the point of two decades ago. I have every sympathy with labor, but its increased share of the national income should come from the accumulating surplus, the location of which is very clearly indicated from the income tax lists, and not from mulcting the professional and clerical classes scarcely a step now in the economic scale above labor itself. I cannot see that the standard of life for the community as a whole is going to be made higher by taking a vacation and a cook away from the college professor and giving them to the conductor or the bricklayer, while the rich business men get incredibly richer.

Before we leave this phase of the question, let us glance at some of the office workers under the new standard. What mass-production methods have done in the way of deadening routine for the factory workers is too well known for repetition, in spite of much glossing over, but what is going on in office work may be less generally understood. The new idea of the relations between employer and employee in mass-production is that the employer buys "production," that is, "output," from the employee. Thus we read in a book on office technic how improvement was made in an up-to-date office. Motion pictures were taken of the clerks opening the morning mail. As a result of a study of these pictures, the motions of the clerks were "reduced from thirteen to six and the output increased from 100 pieces an hour to 200 an hour. A further refinement in the manner of arranging the opened and unopened letters on the table brought the rate to 250 an hour. Output was still further increased by the use of a 'motion-studied table' to 300 an hour."

Stenographers, of course, have been included in this speeding-up process. We read that "in measuring production of this kind several systems are in use. One is that of measuring production by the square inch, with a transparent celluloid, but in most cases a cyclometer is used, which is attached to the machine and records the number of strokes." Production is counted by "points," each "point" being equal to a certain number of strokes, and pay is given accordingly. 250 strokes are deducted for an ordinary error and 1275 strokes for an error on the envelope. 10,000 strokes are added for "a perfect desk," that is one on which, every minute of the week, every implement is so placed as to permit of the greatest speed. Medals and vacation allowances are given for records, and contests are held—though, as to these last, the expert admits that "as a general rule, office contests are not to be recommended. Spurts of speed of any kind are bound to have their reactions and the contest is *often succeeded by a certain amount of lethargy after the goal has been won.* [Italics mine.] But for clearing out an accumulation of work or to rouse the office force they may be very effective." One rubs one's eyes and wonders whether he is reading about America under the highest standard of living ever attained or England at the beginning of the Industrial Revolution. Stenographers share in the high standard to the extent of from $1250 to $1700 a year.

VI

It would be possible to go on almost indefinitely listing our by-products. For example, having everything from furniture to buildings always of the latest is doing away with a whole range of human emotions. When I was at Yale in 1898 I lived in a new dormitory then one year old. Twenty years later when I went back to see what memories the old place might bring to me, I found that the dormitory had been torn down and replaced by a "modern" building. Our schools and their furnishings, altered or rebuilt every few years, make an Eton or a Harrow look painfully shabby perhaps and "unprogressive"; but the boy who sits at the same desk where Shelley or Byron or Chatham or Gladstone or Wellington sat, or lives in their rooms, will dream dreams and gain an inspiration never afforded by the latest efficient furniture from Michigan. It is the law of compensation at work, and what is gained is not always better than what is lost. So far, what has been gained under the high standard is mostly material and what has been lost is mostly spiritual.

It might be thought that with a really high standard, the extra nerve strain of life would be compensated for by extra opportunity for rest, leisure, and quiet, but exactly the reverse is the case. There is less leisure, except perhaps for the old poor and the new very rich, than there was twenty years ago. It is also infinitely harder than it was to find any quiet spot in the country at possible cost to which one can retire to rest one's tired mind and soul. The automobile offers an instructive example of how an end can be defeated by its apparent means. When there were few cars they afforded people a chance to get away into the peace of the

[56]

country, but now their very numbers have ruined the quiet of the countryside. People motor out of the big cities for quiet, only to find that they themselves, multiplied by thousands, have killed the very thing they sought. Recently I inquired of a surgeon who had gone to his house in the country a hundred miles from New York if he had come back rested. He replied emphatically that he had not, and that his place was ruined by people who raced their motor boats with engines unmuffled and made it noisier than even his house in town. As to what will be the condition when aeroplanes become really common, one shudders to think.

Is it any wonder that as other by-products the statisticians tell us that the age of marriage is steadily being postponed, with all that that implies physiologically and psychologically, that the birth rate is falling, that heart disease, divorce, and insanity are all increasing? As we contemplate these and other by-products we may well ask, what makes a high standard of life rather than of living? Granted that we now have billionaires where even millionaires were relatively scarce a generation ago, that labor has risen a little farther above the subsistence level, and that science has given us innumerable toys and conveniences, has not the gulf in comfort widened infinitely between rich and poor? Are the great mass of professional and intellectual workers and of moderate-salaried people as well off in the things that really count as they were a generation ago? For the common fund of our civilization has the advance, such as it is, in the condition of the laboring class offset the comparative decline in the great and almost forgotten middle-class? Has the nation as a whole gained or lost in contentment, peace of mind, assurance of the future, rational enjoyment, and spiritual as well as material comfort? Is it worth while to be continually driven to meet the rent, life insurance, the installments on one's purchases, in order that big business may declare its billions in stock dividends?

There are evidences that a great change may be in prospect. Mass-production requires a steady and enormous flow of sales. On the one hand, the jaded buyers are showing signs of restiveness and of becoming tired of wasting their lives in buying, buying, buying, and paying, paying, paying. They have to be whipped into it by more and more expensive salesmanship. On the other hand, office and sales forces are getting tired of being speeded up as they compare their share in the high standard with that of the men above them, and have to be whipped by the most improved technical methods into greater and greater activity. And all for what? That mass-production shall not falter or fail. The overhead costs of distribution have become staggering. If the public begins to economize and does not buy, then we are told that mass-production will fall down and in the crash to follow no one will have money with which to buy anything. Better than that, we are told, is to buy what we do not really want or cannot afford.

There is no rest from the effort to make money in ever larger and larger amounts. There is no prospect of comfortable retirement in old age. For many who never thought of it in the old days there is the ever-present spectre of illness or incapacity. As has been said, our prosperity can be maintained only by making people want more, and work more, all the time. Those, and they are many, who believe that our recent prosperity has been mainly caused by the phenomenal expansion of the automobile business tell us

[58]

that it will soon be necessary to find some other article which will similarly take the public fancy and create billions of sales—and billions of expense to men already tired of doing nothing but meeting new expenses.

"The highest standard of living ever attained in the history of the world"?

CHAPTER III
OUR DISSOLVING ETHICS

OUR DISSOLVING ETHICS

I

The scapegoat is one of the most venerable and widespread of human institutions. The victim may be literally a goat, as among the Children of Israel, or a rat or a monkey or other animal. Not infrequently it is a human being. For example, among some tribes in Africa all persons who during the year have committed incendiarism, witchcraft, theft, adultery, or other crimes, chip in about ten dollars each and buy a young girl, who is then dragged to the river and drowned for the sins of the town. The sense of guilt requires some sort of expiation, and this "cash and carry" system of expiating the sins of an entire community by attributing them to someone else has obvious advantages. It enables one to settle with one's conscience and the social conventions with a minimum of personal inconvenience and mental anguish.

Here in these United States in this post-war period, realizing that all is not right with our world, we have found the scapegoat which permits us to go about our business with a free mind. The name on its collar is "The Younger Generation." The absurdity of believing that the older generation is not responsible for shaping the conditions which have surrounded the younger, and that a world of mature men and women is being set topsy-turvy by young persons but recently emancipated from the nursery, seems to occur to no one. The hen which hatches a duckling from the egg which some person has set under her unsuspecting wings may well disclaim responsibility for the thoroughly disreputable habits —from the standpoint of a hen—developed by her hatch, but can the older human generation so easily disclaim its responsibility? They may deny it individually and take refuge in the theory that the individual is powerless to counteract the social forces of his time, but this way of escape is as much open to the berated young as to the berating elders. As a matter of fact, whatever we may say of the individual of either generation, I think the responsibility of the older as a whole to the younger as a whole is—to use a liquid measure—just about in the ratio of dad's quart bottle to son's half-pint flask.

That youth is questioning the validity of our entire system of ethics to an extent that is perturbing to parents and, in a lesser degree, to grandparents may be admitted. But it cannot be so readily argued that the babies born between 1900 and 1910 all received a hypodermic injection of new original sin. The most distinguishing characteristic of modern thought is its use of the genetic method. We explain the present by the light of the past. We are most of us evolutionists, except when it comes to the supposed iniquity of youth. But in fact is there any break? Is not the present attitude of youth toward ethical questions the direct and inevitable outcome of what has been going on in our mental world for not one but many generations? That it is so seems true to the author, who also feels that the salvation for society lies in at least a questioning attitude on the part of the new generation.

When we speak of the attitude of youth toward ethics we mean by ethics those general ideas and rules that govern the individual in the practical conduct of his or her life. These have always, in the main, had two sanctions to assist in making them pass current without being questioned by most people. One of these sanctions has been religion and the other the public opinion of the particular class or group to which the individual belonged. Backed by these sanctions, ethical ideas and codes of conduct tend to become fixed, but they are in reality never absolutely fixed. The forms may for long remain the same, but in private conduct the individual, while still outwardly conforming, may cease to be governed by them. Like the dollar, they may remain the standard of value, but their own value—that is, their purchasing power in happiness and human good—may come to vary greatly. The form, however, will not be generally questioned so long as the sanctions behind it are not brought seriously into question.

In the youth of the older generation—that is, let us say, in the decade of the 1880's—the sanctions of the established system of ethics, although being undermined, were still standing firm, to all appearance. These were the religious one of a belief in the Bible as the inspired word of God to be taken literally, and the social one of a code of conduct that belonged to the feudal rather than the industrial phase of society. It is true that Darwin had been writing for twenty years, but such a book as Mrs. Ward's *Robert Elsmere* was considered too dangerous for young people to read, and, although the Industrial Revolution had occurred, woman's sphere in the only classes that were supposed to count in those days was still the home. Very few girls went to college, and even for them the intellectual problems set were not particularly disquieting. The individual youth of either sex may not have been religious or consciously interested in the social sanction for ethical ideas, but on the other hand there was nothing in upbringing or education to make them seriously question the accepted code and standards. Theoretically, that the Bible said "thou shalt not" or that one's group frowned was pretty generally a sufficient guide to conduct. What, in practice, that conduct may have been only the memories of the older generation can reveal.

II

However unquestioningly the average boy or girl of the 1880's may have accepted the traditional views of ethics in relation to the world, many forces of different sorts had long been operative which almost before a new generation should be born were going to blow the old world to bits and create a new one so different as to be almost unrecognizable. That the old ethics and the old sanctions should in all respects have fitted nicely in all the adjustments with that new world is surely too much to expect. And if they did not fit, the only thing to do was to face that fact and try to work out some new adjustment between ideals of conduct and the new environment. It is that need which the older generation has for the most part refused to recognize but which has been recognized by the younger, in many cases heedlessly, but in many more cases seriously, sanely, bravely.

That there may be need for a revaluation of our ethics is obvious to them. Why should it be to them and not to so many of their elders? For one thing, these youngsters have been fed on a different intellectual fare from that on which their parents were fed. It must not be lost to sight, however, that this fare has been prepared for them by their parents, or at least by their elders. It must also be noted that they are receiving instruction in enormously increased numbers. College is no longer for the exceptional man only, socially or intellectually. Young men of all grades, and, what is more important, young women also, are going to college by the hundreds of thousands annually. The responsibility for what happens to them there intellectually is squarely up to the older generation. The institutions are provided and run by that generation, the young are in great measure sent by it, and the instruction is almost wholly provided by it.

Before we pass on to consider the intellectual environment of the younger generation, we may note another point with regard to the general atmosphere which has been provided for it by the older. That atmosphere is one of intense absorption in the material basis of life. The older generation has lost its spiritual bearings by its mad scramble for money at any spiritual cost in order to pay for the so-called high standard of living which, to a great extent, has been due to lack of character, that character which enables a person to perceive clearly what is for his genuine good and to reject what is not as forcibly as the body tries to reject poison. The high standard is, in most of its aspects, a high standard on a low plane, and to a considerable extent it has been made possible because people have given up using their energies and resources to attain to any standard on the higher plane. Having, with all the accumulated resources of a wealthy and powerful civilization, devoted their energies to the easier task of elaborating their life on the lower, the material plane, it is little wonder that they have achieved "the highest standard" *on that plane* the world has seen.

[67]

But by devoting all their energies to the elaboration and piling up of things, to the making of the possession of things a necessity of their lives, a symbol of success and a basis of personal appraisal, they have brought about a situation in which the obtaining of money in quantities wholly unnecessary for a sane ordering of life has become the overwhelming preoccupation of their minds. The softness of intellectual fibre that makes the search for material good so much easier than the search for spiritual, that lack of character that makes us easy victims of the opinions and standards of others, that lack of resisting power that makes us the victims of any advertising expert or persuasive salesman, that fear of mass opinion, that love of luxury which is always insidious and which grows by what it feeds upon,—all combine to make us believe that we are rising to a higher life when we are in reality losing that life in a complete devoting of ourselves to the mere machinery of life.

Man always attempts to rationalize any position he assumes, and to give high-sounding motives to what may in reality stem from the basest. Because we choose to make making money our main preoccupation, we call it service. Because we choose to put off the day when the nation shall turn to other things, we say "America is young." Because we choose to yield to the seduction of every new toy and luxury, we claim that we are establishing a "high standard of living." Because we cannot resist giving ourselves everything, we say that we devote ourselves to our mad rush for money in order that we may give our children everything, regardless of the fact that by raising their standard of income and needs, and lowering their standard of life, we are in reality making their future infinitely more difficult for them.

The ethics of the older generation have dissolved in part
from the hypocrisy that has been bred in it by this desire for
money and what it will bring in luxury and social consideration. The dissolution is evident not only in our having
become a nation of speculators who are forever trying to get
something for nothing, not merely in the defalcations and
greater or lesser crimes committed by the weaker, but in that
more subtle crime against our higher natures, and against
the new generation, the crime of cloaking our weakness and
material desires in the guise of a "high standard" and of
"giving our children everything."

Let us consider further a few of the ideas which are familiar
to the younger generation and which to a great extent were
not so to the youth of the older one. For one thing, we may
cite the comparative study of religion. There are only two
methods of intellectual approach to any subject, whether
religious or scientific. We may rely upon authority—that is,
someone else's judgment—or upon our own. From the time
that Protestantism rejected the authority of the Catholic
Church and insisted upon the right of personal searching
and interpretation of the Scriptures the way was opened for
the decline in the prestige of authority. (I may say that I
am not a Catholic.) Of course particular sects could establish new creeds and try to set up new authority in the place
of old; and because man is not wholly a logical creature, and
because most men still believed in the verbal inspiration of
the Bible however they chose to interpret it, this served to
maintain its authority until almost the present day. With
the rise, however, of the higher criticism, and more particularly the study of comparative religion, the religious sanction
for ethics received a severe blow. For one young person who

bothers to read a textual criticism of any Biblical book, numbers are familiar with and delight in Frazer's *Golden Bough*. Nothing serves more subtly to break down a belief in the theology of Christianity than to find, for example, that the idea of a dying god is common to many religions and many people, that likewise is the idea of an immaculate conception or a virgin birth, and that even the doctrine of transubstantiation and the eating of bread which somehow becomes the body of a god is widespread. The question naturally arises why, if we must reject these doctrines as taught by every religion except Christianity, should we be obliged to accept them as true in that? Religion and theology are very different things. The younger generation are not irreligious. In the truest sense they want a religion, but they do not want as a substitute the theology preached by many clergymen or the mere husk of social service given in so many churches in place of both theology and religion. It is my experience that many boys and girls who cannot be induced to go to church are more genuinely religious than the clergyman who bewails the fact that they will not come to hear him preach. But for them a mere sentence in the Bible can no longer be appealed to as affording a sufficient sanction for an ethical idea or a code of conduct that has no other apparent reason for being.

In another comparative study, that of anthropology, they also find much to make them question current ethics. By a study of the various tribes and races of the world in different times and places the student finds that they all, indeed, have codes and ethics, but that these all vary and have grown out of specific social or economic needs under particular conditions. The institution of the family, for example, and the relations of the sexes have assumed many forms. The whole question is thrown into the intellectual melting pot as one for discussion, and the sanction tends to become not some religious authority but the good of society and the individual. The older generation was taught that God gave certain commands, regarding sexual and other relations, engraved on a tablet of stone, to a Hebrew some thousands of years ago. It is useless to tell that to a young person to-day and expect it to settle the matter.

If he turns to philosophy he comes in contact with a world, not of fixed ideas, of eternal verities, but a world where all is in a state of flux. It is not that certain "eternal truths" are being attacked in order to substitute others in their places, but that the lasting validity of truths, any truths, is itself under fire. No teacher, perhaps, has been more popular or exerted greater influence than the late William James, and the pragmatism associated with his name is, in the form of its presentation at least, one of the original American contributions to philosophy. Now the essence of pragmatism is that the truth or validity of an idea depends on whether it works in practice. "The truest scientific hypothesis," he says in one of his most popular books, "is that which, as we say, 'works best'; and it can be no otherwise with religious hypotheses." For the reader to add "ethical hypotheses" is to take an obvious step. Again he says: "The true . . . is only the expedient in the way of our thinking, just as the right is only the expedient in the way of our behaving." It is true that he adds "expedient in the long run and on the whole," but if the true and the right can only be tested by their working it is evident that, as the world is made up of in-

[71]

dividuals, the only experimental tests possible must be made by individuals.

This philosophy is thoroughly consonant with the American temperament and natural outlook on life. We are not mentally a subtle or an abstract people. If a thing does not work, it is of no use. If it does, that is a sufficient answer to any attack, and it is this pragmatic sanction that, consciously or not, many a thoughtful young person of to-day is seeking for the new ethics. In the writings of the most influential living American philosopher, John Dewey, he again finds this sense of fluidity in life and thought. "The first distinguishing characteristic of thinking is facing the facts," says Dewey, in words which appeal to one of the finest sides of the young people. Dewey as an ardent evolutionist, and a disbeliever in any fixed forms or species, holds out as the hope for the future—and disagreement with him would seem to plunge us in hopeless pessimism—that human nature is not unchangeable, that there is possibility of unlimited alteration by change in the environment, and that this change may be brought about by taking conscious thought and not awaiting the slow alteration of nature. This again throws open the way for a serious consideration as to whether, if we can change the environment and human nature,—and both *have* been enormously changed,—we keep unchanged codes of conduct.

Philosophical and scientific ideas are coming to affect the thinking of people, who may never read the books in which they are primarily expressed, with steadily increasing acceleration. It took many generations for the discovery by Copernicus that the earth was not the centre of the universe, but moved round the sun, to affect religious and other ideas.

It took something more than a generation for Darwin's theory of evolution to revolutionize all our thinking. Who knows what the influence, not merely in science, but in all social thinking, including ethics, may very soon be of Einstein's theory of relativity? It has already had great influence, in spite of the fact that those of us who are not mathematicians cannot comprehend it. But to be told—to mention only one aspect of his theory—that there is no such thing as a "correct size" of anything, but that for human knowledge the size of anything depends on the relative speed maintained by the observer and the thing observed, is, literally, appalling. This fact brings to us in startling fashion and in mathematical terms the realization that things are not absolute but relative. The theory of relativity is far more of a solvent for the eternal verities than either the Copernican or the Darwinian theory, and its effect, already being felt, is bound to be profound in realms of thought seemingly remote from physics.

III

In a few words, the young generation has a religion, but it is nebulous. It may to some extent serve, at moments when it is felt, as a source of strength, as an aid to being straight and decent. At many times it is not felt. In any case it issues no commands covering specific conduct. It has no decalogue, and the question of what is decent and straight is left open by it. The youngster's ethics, therefore, have no religious sanction which points out any specific rules of conduct. On the other hand, through his anthropological and sociological studies he comes to realize that there are innumerable ways of living and choices of conduct, all of which have been or are thought right and moral by some people, sometime, somewhere. What constitutes right conduct depends, therefore, apparently on conditions and not on any eternal rules. The prevailing temperament of his nation and its most popular philosophy teach him that the only test of validity is "work-ability"—that if an idea has good results it is good, if it has not it is bad. The world has never been a very satisfactorily organized place, and nowadays, what with the results of the war, our socially developed conscience, and all the conditions of present life, it can hardly be said to look like an outstanding success. Those who have lived long have for the most part become either reconciled or hopeless over the situation. But for the young it is different, fortunately. They see the poverty, the social injustice, the frequent emotional maladjustment between the individual and society, and they do not see, and let us hope that they are right, that such things need always be.

The ethics of the older person do not change. He too may have, as he probably has, lost the religious sanction, but as the twig is bent the tree has grown. He was taught so and so and he sticks to it, and anything else seems wrong. Moreover, he has learned that one cannot meet every moral emergency by thinking it out as a unique case. Life is short, emergencies come suddenly, and one must have some general rules to guide. He is accustomed to the old rules, it is his habit to obey them, and he simplifies his life by continuing to do so. The youngster, however, has no ready-made adjustments and is intensely interested in life, and willing to take time and risks. His entire education has taught him to take a scientific view of life, and to reject mere authority.

It is not enough for a parent to point out that something is "right" or "wrong." The youth asks "Why?" The only satisfactory answer is one that will convince him that a certain line of conduct will or will not conduce to his own good or that of society.

With the education which we give to youth, I do not see how we could expect any other result. The fact is that the younger generation is simply carrying forward where we leave off. The decay in belief in the Christian theology, the loss of religious sanction for ethics, the development of such comparative studies as religion and anthropology, the pragmatic philosophy, the Freudian psychology of inhibitions and complexes, and the various scientific and mechanical discoveries which have transformed the world, have all been the work of the older generation. The youth who are coming forward to-day receive the full force of all this straight in the face and all at once. And the changes are coming faster and faster.

Personally I do not see how we can quarrel with the general ideas that the younger generation has as to its ethical problem—that is, that there is no indubitable religious or other authoritarian sanction for any specific rules of conduct; that different ethical codes have best suited different peoples, times, and conditions; that the best test of any hypothesis is whether it will work; and that in a world in flux there is no reason for positing and insisting upon an eternally fixed code of ethics. We do know that such codes will gradually alter in any case. The question is whether it is possible to use intelligence in altering them or whether we have to trust to the slow process of an unintelligent alteration. If they do gradually get adjusted to new social conditions and structures, then it is reasonable to suppose that such an adjustment should bear some time relation to the rapidity of change in society. With the increasing speeding up both of thought and of scientific discovery, the rate of change in society is also speeding up enormously. Unless we can assist intelligently the process of adjusting ethical ideas and codes to the social change, the amount of injustice and individual maladjustments, emotional, economic, and other, may increase so rapidly as to endanger the social structure itself.

The economic independence of the younger generation of women has already profoundly altered the whole family relation and that of the two sexes. The motor car, whether one likes it or not, has almost equally altered the whole question of the supervision of the two sexes at an earlier stage. Again, whether one likes it or not, the scientific investigations now being carried on in several parts of the world into the question of methods of birth control may have still more profound effects within the lifetime of the coming generation. The changes which have come already since the Industrial Revolution and the harnessing of steam are probably nothing to what we may expect within the next generation if the present rate of discovery and alteration continues. To say that rules of personal conduct established under sanctions which no longer exist for most people, and for conditions which have already been changed almost beyond recognition, must last unaltered forever is simply to refuse to see the facts and to court disaster, individual or social.

Our ethics and their old sanctions are already in dissolution. That has been accomplished by the older, not the younger, generation. What the younger generation and their children may be called upon to do may be to make the most rapid, far-reaching, and consciously intelligent readjustment of ethical ideas to altered social structure that the race has ever been called upon to make. We of the older generation have played with ideas and let loose forces the power of which we little dreamed of. We have, indeed, sowed the wind, and it will be those of the younger generation who will reap the whirlwind unless they can control it. Individually we may feel guiltless. We may merely have been busy with out intellectual hobbies, our money-getting, our loving and striving, but we surely cannot lay the blame for the intellectual or moral conditions upon the scapegoat of the "Younger Generation." To condemn them and regard ourselves complacently is as unjust as it is unwarranted. They have inherited, perhaps, the biggest mess and biggest problem that was ever bequeathed by one generation to another. Never has the road been wilder or the signposts fewer.

We may address the young in the words of FitzJames Stephen: "Each must act as he thinks best; and if he is wrong, so much the worse for him. We stand on a mountain pass in the midst of whirling snow and blinding mist, through which we get glimpses now and then of paths which may be deceptive. If all stand still we shall be frozen to death. If we take the wrong road we shall be dashed to pieces. We do not certainly know whether there is any right one. What must we do? "Be strong and of a good courage." Act for the best, hope for the best, and take what comes. If death ends all, we cannot meet death better."

But if that is all the injunction we can give them, are we performing our duty, and can we blame them, instead of ourselves, if they take the wrong road, or if death ends all?

We of the older generation believe both from education in youth and from the experiences of our lives that there are certain values in life. In our minds they have the sanctions of tradition and experience. The new generation has no experience and declines to accept mere tradition. Is it not the duty of the older generation to face the problem, both for its own sake and that of the young, and seriously to attempt to arrive at some reasonable philosophy of life that shall validate the values it believes in?

Is it not the plain truth that in all too many cases the older generation has had both its intellectual and its moral fibre sapped by its own mad desire to make money? While paying lip service to the old values of life, which it repeats, without being able to produce any sanction for them, to the young, has it itself lived according to those values or has it not abandoned them for the sake of piling up riches? In the past forty years have the ethics of the counting room, the office, the factory, and the legislatures been those of the church and the drawing room? Has the older generation lived soberly, has it spent sanely, has it lived chastely, has it preferred the spiritual to the material things of life, has it refrained from bribing policemen and legislatures, has it voted from principle, has it tried to insist upon honesty in its public servants, has it tried to cultivate its mind and taste, has it tried honestly to think things through and attain a sound philosophy of living that it may pass on to its children? These questions to a great extent answer themselves. They are not put to absolve the younger generation from responsibility but from blame. In the moulding of character, example, after all, is perhaps of more importance than moral saws or authoritative sanctions. When the older generation looks at the younger it is looking in the mirror at itself. It is itself, only far from the safe shelter of home, straying inexperienced on the "mountain pass in the midst of whirling snow and blinding mist." Would the younger generation be out in the storm so utterly without guidance, if the older had not devoted its time, strength and mental energy to the gaining of wealth and luxury instead of to the values of a sane and humane life?

CHAPTER IV
JEFFERSON AND HAMILTON
TO-DAY

JEFFERSON AND HAMILTON TO-DAY

I

"We hold these truths to be self-evident,—that all men are created equal; that they are endowed by their Creator with certain inalienable rights; that among these are Life, Liberty, and the pursuit of Happiness."

—JEFFERSON

"The People, your People, Sir, is a great Beast."

—HAMILTON

Rhetoric and sentimentalism have always appealed almost equally to the American people. "Waving the flag" and "sob stuff" are the two keys which unlock the hearts of our widest publics. It is not, therefore, perhaps wholly unfair to take the most rhetorical and emotional of the utterances of Jefferson and Hamilton with relation to their fundamental political philosophies to head this article. The complete divergence of the two men could be shown in many quotations more carefully worded, but would appear only the more clearly. That divergence was sharp-cut and complete. Their views as to the relation of the people at large to government were as far asunder as the poles. In examining the writings of both these statesmen, it has been borne in upon me that if, as Lincoln said, a nation cannot live half slave and half free, neither can it live half Hamilton and half Jefferson, especially when the two ingredients are mixed, as they now are, in the blurred mentalities of the same individuals.

The two men themselves knew this well in their own lifetimes. Each fought valiantly for his own beliefs. Each felt that one or the other, and one philosophy or the other, must conquer. Neither believed that the two could lie down together, lion and lamb, in that curious and conglomerately furnished mental apartment, the American consciousness. That this has come to be the case merely shows for how little ideas really count in modern American political life, a life which is almost wholly emotional and financial rather than intellectual. Ideas are supposed to be explosive. In America, apparently, they are as harmless as "duds." Even the Civil War, our greatest "moral" struggle, was largely a matter of emotion; and as for the last war, anyone who, like myself, was in a position to watch the manufacture of propaganda can say whether it was directed to the heart or to the head of the multitude.

There are certain ways in which conflicting ideas may be held in the one community without hypocrisy. In every age, for example, there has been one set of beliefs for the learned, the cultivated, and the sophisticated, and another for the mob. The mob in the past was never educated, and even "the people" to-day, in spite of a smattering of "book knowledge," are not educated in the same way that the cultivated and, in an uninvidious sense, the privileged classes are. Here and there one may find a case of a mechanic, a farmer, a saleslady, or what not who really uses his or her mind, but how rare the cases are I leave to anyone who is not afraid to come out and tell the truth as he has found it, speaking broadly. Merely reading a newspaper, even if not of the tabloid variety, or tucking away unrelated bits of information uncritically, is not thinking. Between the man who critically analyzes, compares, and thinks, and the one who merely reads, there is a great gulf fixed as to ideas.

Such a case has always been common in religion, from the medicine man or the Egyptian priest down to the Archbishop of Canterbury or a cardinal in Rome. The dogmas of the Christian religion, for example, as held by the two latter are quite different "ideas" from the same as held by a person who has had no philosophical training and who could not if he would, and would not if he could, undertake the course of study necessary to get the point of view of the bishop or the cardinal. In this sense, ideas which are so different as to be almost, if not quite, contradictory may nevertheless live on side by side in the same society without hypocrisy. They may, indeed, be considered as expressions of the same idea merely attuned differently to be caught, as far as possible, by minds of different "pitch."

Again, we may have ideals which apparently conflict with the practice of society, but they *are* ideals and, however far practice may fall short of attainment, there is no real conflict, because in fact a certain amount of effort, however slight and however sporadic, is made to attain them. The conflict is not between clashing ideas or ideals, but between ideal and practice.

Once more, contradictory ideas may exist in the same society without hypocrisy if they are held by different individuals or parties who openly avow them and who either honestly agree to differ in peace or who struggle to get one or the other set of ideas accepted by all.

But the odd thing about the contradictory Hamilton-

Jefferson ideas is that they are not held by different social classes,—the one set of ideas as a sort of esoteric doctrine and the other publicly proclaimed,—nor are they any longer the platforms of two parties, as in the days when the two statesmen themselves fought honestly, courageously, and bitterly for them in the open. And I say this even though the portrait of Hamilton may adorn the walls of Republican clubs and that of Jefferson those of the Democratic ones. The present situation is anomalous.

Hamilton and Jefferson each had a fundamental premise. These were as utterly contradictory as two major premises could possibly be. From each of these respectively each of the men deduced his system of government with impeccable logic. Yet what of these men and their philosophies in our politics to-day? There is scarcely a politician of any party who would dare to preach Hamilton's main deductions, while not a single one could be elected to any office if he did not preach Jefferson's premise. The Republicans claim to be followers of Hamilton, yet they would not dare to preach Hamilton's most fundamental assumption, that on which his whole structure was based. The Democrats claim to be followers of Jefferson, yet they have departed far from some of his most important deductions. On the whole, I confess I think they show the greater intellectual integrity of the two parties, yet, so far, I have always voted Republican, which is a sample of the intellectual muddle our politics are in.

II

Before going further, let us examine very briefly what the ideas of the two men were.

Jefferson's fundamental idea, his major premise, was an utter trust in the morality, the integrity, the ability, and the political honesty of the common man of America, at least as America was then and as Jefferson hoped it would remain for centuries. He made this point again and again, and from it deduced his whole system. Based on that belief, he wrought out the doctrine that the only safety for the State depended on the widest possible extension of the franchise. "The influence over government must be shared among all the people. If every individual which composes their mass participates of the ultimate authority, the government will be safe." "It is rarely that the public sentiment decides immorally or unwisely." "It has been thought that corruption is restrained by confining the right of suffrage to a few of the wealthier of the people; but it would be more effectually restrained by an extension of that right to such numbers as would bid defiance to the means of corruption." He dreaded the power of wealth, the growth of manufacturers, the development of banks, the creation of a strong central government, a judiciary which was not elected and readily amenable to the will of the majority. He wished for as little government as possible, with few hampering restrictions on the individual expression of the citizen. He was for free trade and universally diffused free education. He wished to preserve the State governments in all their vigor, which, at that time, meant practically independent and sovereign commonwealths. To the Federal government he would allot the most meagre of functions, merely those dealing with foreign nations and concerning such acts in common as it would be impracticable for the states to perform individually. His ideal was "a wise and frugal government, which shall restrain men from injuring one another, shall leave them otherwise free to regulate their own pursuits of industry and improvement, and shall not take from the mouth of labor the bread it has earned." "This," he added, "is the sum of good government."

On the other hand, let us turn to Hamilton. The remark prefixed to this article, although made in a moment of vexation, expresses his attitude toward the common people, whom he never trusted. In his writings for the public, he had, of course, to be more discreet in his utterances, but his statements, and still more his acts, are clear enough. "Take mankind as they are, and what are they governed by? Their passions. . . . One great error is that we suppose mankind more honest than they are." "It is a just observation that the people commonly *intend* the *public good*. This often applies to their very errors. But their good sense would despise the adulator who should pretend that they always *reason right* about the *means* of promoting it. . . . When occasions present themselves, in which the interests of the people are at variance with their inclinations, it is the duty of the persons whom they have appointed to be the guardians of those interests, to withstand the temporary delusions." "The voice of the people has been said to be the voice of God; and, however generally this maxim has been quoted and believed, it is not true to fact. The people are turbulent and changing; they seldom judge right or determine right." "Can a democratic Assembly, who annually revolve in the mass of the people, be supposed steadily to pursue the public good?" "The difference [between rich and poor] indeed consists not in the quantity, but kind of vices, which are incident to the various classes; and here the advantage of character belongs to the wealthy. Their vices are probably more favorable to the prosperity of the State than those of the indigent, and partake less of moral depravity." "It is an unquestionable truth, that the body of the people in every country desire sincerely its prosperity. But it is equally unquestionable that they do not possess the discernment and stability necessary for systematic government."

As a corollary from this fundamental assumption, Hamilton devoted all his great abilities to the development of as strong a central government as possible. He would remove power as completely as might be from the hands of the common people and place it in those who had inherited or acquired wealth and position. For this purpose he deliberately set about to tie the wealthy classes to government by his Funding Act, by the creation of manufactures, by a protective tariff, by the establishment of banks, and in other ways. He felt that human nature had always been the same and would not change. Public education did not interest him. His one interest was the establishment of a strong government in strong hands, and he evidently felt that a smattering of book knowledge, such as our people even yet get in grade and high schools, would not alter their characters and make them safe depositaries for political power. In fact, and this is an important point to note in his system, the development of the industrial state would tend to make the people at large even less capable than in his day by creating, as it has done, a vast mass of mere wage-earners, floating city dwellers, on the one hand, while it built up his wealthy class on the other. The great mass of the people, he reasoned, would always have to be governed in any case, and the more powerful and influential the wealthy could be made, the stronger would they be for governing. Out of these simple assumptions, the banks, the vast "implied powers" of the central government, the funding of the national debt, the rise of a manufacturing industry, and the formation of a tariff designed not merely to protect infant industries but to create a dependence of wealth upon government favor, were developed as clearly and logically as a theorem in Euclid.

Thus, very briefly, and perhaps a trifle crudely, we have stated the real bases of Jeffersonianism and Hamiltonianism. Their whole systems of government sprang logically from their differing premises. Jefferson trusted the common man. Hamilton deeply distrusted him. That was a very clear-cut issue from 1790 to 1800, and both men, and the people themselves, recognized it as such. Stupendous consequences would follow from the success in practical politics at that time of either of those theories of human nature. For the first decade of our national life Hamilton beat Jefferson in practical politics, and in a very real sense created the United States as we know it to-day, a vast manufacturing nation with its Federal government eating up all the state governments like an Aaron's rod, with its trusts and its money power and its Chinese wall of a protective tariff, and all the rest. There is no doubt of the strength of the present government. There is no doubt of the support it derives from the wealthy classes. There is no doubt of the colossal success of the industrial experiment as a creator of wealth.

The Republican Party may well look back to Hamilton as its High Priest, but the odd thing is that Hamilton created all this heritage of strength and power and banks and tariffs for a very simple reason, and that reason the Republican Party would not dare to breathe aloud in any party convention, campaign, or speech. "The People, your People, Sir, is a great Beast." Imagine that as an exordium of a keynote speech to nominate Calvin Coolidge or Herbert Hoover. Hamilton deliberately set about to create special privileges for certain classes so that those classes would in turn support the government and control the people. What does the Republican Party do? It hangs on for dear life to all those special privileges, it preaches Hamilton's corollaries as the one pure political gospel, and then it steals Jefferson's major premise, and preaches the wisdom and the nobility and the political acumen of the common people! One feels like inquiring in the vernacular, with deep emotion, "How did you get that way?" As when watching a prestidigitator, one's jaw drops with amazement as the rabbit pops from the one hat we could not possibly have expected it from.

On the other hand, how about the Democrats? They too preach Jefferson's major premise—the wisdom, the ability, and the political acumen of the common people. But what have they done with most of Jefferson's deductions? They certainly do not evince any strong desire to reduce the functions of government and bring it down to that "wise and frugal" affair their leader visioned. They are more inclined to increase government bureaus and supervision and interference with the affairs of the citizen. As to the tariff, they have capitulated completely and in the last campaign scarcely mentioned the dangerous topic, for fear of losing money and votes. They preach their founder's major premise and hurrah for the common people, but beyond that I cannot penetrate at all through the murky fog which hides all real political issues in the United States to-day.

[91]

There is the vague sense of expectancy one has during the entr'acte at the theatre. There is nothing to see, but eventually the curtain will go up again. Meanwhile the scene shifters are supposedly busy. I have an idea that before long the scene-shifters will not be our spineless politicians, but the Fates.

III

And now, lastly, let us consider one more curious thing about this preaching and living of Hamilton's conclusions illogically from Jefferson's premise.

Is that premise really valid to-day for either party? Would even Jefferson believe it to be? There is no telling what he would say if he came back, but it must be remembered that he did not believe in the common people always and under all circumstances. He drew a distinction many times between those living in the simple agricultural America of his time and those in the crowded cities of Europe. In a long and interesting letter to John Adams, he wrote: "Before the establishment of the United States, nothing was known to history but the man of the old world, crowded within limits either small or overcharged, and steeped in the vices which that situation generates. A government adapted to such men would be one thing; but a very different one, that for the man of these States. Here every one may have land to labor for himself, if he chooses; or, preferring the exercise of any other industry, may exact from it such compensation as not only to afford comfortable subsistence, but wherewith to provide for a cessation from labor in old age. . . . Such men may safely and advantageously reserve to themselves a wholesome control over their public affairs, and a degree of

[92]

freedom, which, in the hands of the *canaille* of the cities of Europe, would be instantly perverted to the demolition and destruction of everything public and private." Again he says that our governments will surely become corrupt when our conditions as to crowded cities shall have approximated those of the Europe of his day.

Without here attempting to pass any judgment on the success of Hamilton's work in its human rather than its financial and governmental aspects, we shall have to admit that it has brought about the very conditions which Jefferson dreaded and under which he feared that his common man would become corrupt and incapable of self-government. The tremendous demand for labor resulted in our importing by the millions those very *canaille*, in Jefferson's phrase,— people from the lowest classes of overcrowded Europe,—in whom he had no confidence whatever, whom he considered incapable of self-government. We have ourselves developed overcrowded conditions. There are three times as many people in the metropolitan area of New York to-day as there were in the entire United States in Jefferson's day. Over fifty per cent of our population now live in cities and are beginning, in the larger ones at least, to develop the vices of a city mentality. In fact the corruption is worse here than in Europe in many respects. London has a larger population than New York, yet it costs $180,000,000 a year to run that city and $525,000,000 to run New York. Even making all allowances for difference in prices, there is no escaping a most unpleasant conclusion from those figures.

Yet Jefferson claimed that if he was right in his assumption that the common man was honest, able, and capable of self-government, the governments most honestly and frugally

[93]

conducted would be those nearest to him, the local rather than the Federal. Jefferson's whole philosophy was agrarian. It was based on the one population in the world he thought worthy of it—a population of which ninety per cent were farmers, mostly owning their own homes. He hoped it would remain so for many hundreds of years and believed that it would. It did so for only a few decades.

How long are we to go on preaching Jefferson and practising Hamilton? Jefferson's philosophy develops from his premise and hangs together. So does Hamilton's. But the two do not mix at all, as both men recognized in deadly earnest. We have been trying to mix them ever since, oratorically at least. We practise Hamilton from January 1 to July 3 every year. On July 4 we hurrah like mad for Jefferson. The next day we quietly take up Hamilton again for the rest of the year as we go about our business. I do not care which philosophy a man adopts, but to preach one and to practise the other is hypocrisy, and hypocrisy in the long run poisons the soul.

Personally I prefer Jefferson as a man to Hamilton. In his spirit I believe he was far more of an aristocrat than Hamilton ever was, with all his social pretensions. I prefer the America which Jefferson visualized and hoped for to that which Hamilton dreamed of and brought to pass on a scale he never could measure. On the other hand, I believe that the future will be, as the past has been, Hamilton's. His hopes and Jefferson's fears have come true. The small farmer, the shopkeeper, the artisan are being more and more crowded out from the interest of a plutocratic government. A Hamiltonian philosophy or government cares nothing for them as compared with the large manufacturer and larger trust.

If we want to know why they should not be helped or protected as well as corporations which can declare hundreds of per cent in stock dividends and then cash dividends on the stock dividends and so on ad infinitum, we must go back to Hamilton and the beginning of his system. I do not see now that any other system is possible. Perhaps some day we may secure a lowering of the tariff to less swinish levels and certain other reforms, but as a whole the system must stand. Jefferson's dream of a new and better world at last opened to men, with a whole continent at their back over which as freeholders they could slowly expand for ages, has passed. We have swallowed our heritage almost at a gulp. We have become as a nation colossally rich. But if anyone thinks we have become more honest or more capable of self-government, let him study the records.

If we are to accept Hamilton's conclusions and system, why not be honest and accept, instead of Jefferson's, his own premise, the only real basis for his conclusions and, as he believed, the only real buttress for his system? That system was based upon the deep, honest, and publicly avowed belief that the people could not govern themselves. That they do so, except to the extent of sometimes impeding action at a crisis, is, I believe, far less true than they believe, unpalatable as that remark may be. Of course, "public opinion" has to be considered, but anyone who knows how public opinion is manufactured can take that at its real value. Of course, again, there is a lot of bunkum talked, but that can also be taken at its real value. There are two passages in "Uncle" Joe Cannon's *Autobiography* that, taken together, are very amusing. In one of the chapters he describes how Mark Hanna had the nomination for President of the United States absolutely in his own hand. The sole choice "the people" had was to vote for or against Hanna's man. Yet Cannon ends his book by saying that America is ruled from the homes and the firesides! As for public opinion, it is far from always being salutary. I have good reason to believe that, had it not been for public opinion in the Middle West, Wilson would have entered the war long before he did; it would have ended far sooner; and the world would have been saved much of all that has happened since. Had it not been for public opinion, which really meant popular emotion, in about twenty countries after the Armistice, the men gathered at Paris to make the Peace Treaty would have been able to make a far more sensible one than they did.

One last point. Hamilton believed in giving special privileges to certain classes so as to secure their adherence and support. That is understandable, and is good Republican doctrine to-day. But those who did not get those privileges were to be kept as far as possible from any control of government. That may sound a bit cold-blooded, but it also is logical and understandable. Jefferson believed in privileges for none and a voice in the government for all. Again, given his premise, that is a logical and understandable position. But where is the logic, and what will happen, when you give the power to all and still try to retain special privileges for some? For a while the patient may be kept quiet with strong doses of "hokum," but some day we may find that the opposing views of the two statesmen of 1800 cannot be fused as innocuously as we have tried to fuse them.

Hamilton and Jefferson. Honest men both, and bitterest of foes in a fight over premises and principles which they knew were fundamental. How amazed they would be could they return and find us preaching the one, practising the other, and mixing their clear-cut positions together! Hamilton might be pleased to see the stupendous growth of all he had dreamed, but would ask why, when all had gone so perfectly according to his plans, political power had been transferred to the people at large. Jefferson would say, why preach theoretically his fundamental assumption and then do all and more than his bitterest foe could do to nullify it practically? Both might say, hypocrites, or addle-pates.

Our apologetic answer for the last century might be—democracy. The answer for the next century is hidden, but is deeply troubling the thoughtful or the wealthy of every nation except the prosperous class in America, which is too gorged with profits to think about anything.

CHAPTER V
OUR LAWLESS HERITAGE

OUR LAWLESS HERITAGE

I

The question is frequently asked, "Is the Eighteenth Amendment making us a nation of lawbreakers?" There are two answers, depending upon the meaning of the question. If it is intended to ask whether many people are disobeying the law and whether the Amendment is helping to break down respect for law itself, the answer is emphatically, yes. If, on the other hand, the question is intended to imply that we were a law-abiding nation before we went dry, the answer is as emphatically, no. Any law that goes counter to the strong feeling of a large part of the population is bound to be disobeyed in America. Any law that is disobeyed inevitably results in lawbreaking and in lowering respect for law as law. The Eighteenth Amendment is doing that on a gigantic scale, but it is operating upon a population already the most lawless in spirit of any in the great modern civilized countries. Lawlessness has been and is one of the most distinctive American traits. It is obvious that a nation does not become lawless or law-abiding overnight. The United States is English in origin, and, even making allowance for the hordes of "foreigners" who have come here, there must be some reason why to-day England is the most law-abiding of nations and ourselves the least so. It is impossible to blame the situation on the "foreigners." The overwhelming mass of them were law-abiding in their native lands. If they become lawless here it must be largely due to the American atmosphere and conditions. There seems to me to be plenty of evidence to prove that the immigrants are made lawless by America rather than that America is made lawless by them. If the general attitude toward law, if the laws themselves and their administration, were all as sound here as in the native lands of the immigrants, those newcomers would give no more trouble here than they did at home. This is not the case, and Americans themselves are, and almost always have been, less law-abiding than the more civilized European nations.

Living much in England, I have already had frequent occasion to note the startling difference which one feels with respect to the public attitude toward law in that country and in our own. No one can be there without feeling this difference, but lest my own insistence upon it be set down to prejudice, let me quote the opinion of Dr. Kirchwey, head of the Department of Criminology in the New York School of Social Work, formerly Dean of the Columbia Law School, and one-time Warden of Sing Sing Prison. "Our visitor to London," he writes, "will have heard much of the low crime rate of that great city, of the efficiency of the unarmed police, of the swift and sure administration of criminal laws. Let him look further and note the ingrained habit of law-observance of every class of the population from the man in the street to the judge on the bench. He will find no attempt made to violate the restrictive laws governing the sale of liquor, whether by licensed vendor or by the customer; rarely a violation of traffic regulations by cabmen or private driver . . . he will not discover a trace of the sporting spirit which leads his fellow-citizens of the American commonwealth to laugh at the escape of a daring criminal from

the legal consequences of his guilt. And, if he cares to pursue
his studies further, he will find on the other side of the
English Channel still other communities where, as in England, a low crime rate is set against a background of an all
but universal sentiment of respect for law and order." How
is it that we in America to-day are without the pale of this
respect for law which is one of the fundamentals of civilization? In seeking an answer we obviously cannot confine
ourselves to the present decade, but must dig deep into the
past. Only parts of the appalling record that we shall find,
when we do so, can be touched upon here.

Respect for law is a plant of slow growth. If, for centuries, laws have been reasonably sound, and impartially
and surely enforced by the lawful authorities, respect for
law as law will increase. If, on the other hand, laws are
unreasonable or go counter to the habits and desires of large
parts of the population, and are not enforced equitably or
surely, respect for law will decrease. On the whole, the first
supposition applies to the history of England for three
hundred years and the second one to our own.

II

Let us consider our colonial period first; and it must be
remembered that we were a part of the British Empire for
a longer period than we have been independent. The way
in which those supposedly godly persons, the leaders of the
Massachusetts theocracy, began at once by breaking the
law of England will help us to an understanding of the whole
colonial situation. The Massachusetts Company, a business
corporation in the eyes of the English Government, applied

for a charter of incorporation and received it. It provided for what we should call voting stockholders and a board of directors to be elected by them. Nothing more was intended in the grant by the Government. Some of the leaders in the company conceived the brilliant idea of secretly carrying the actual charter to America and using it as though it were the constitution of a practically self-governing State. This was done, but the foundation of the strongest of the Puritan colonies was thus tainted with illegality and chicanery from the start. Not only that, but in the beginning even the terms of the charter were not complied with and the government was usurped by the leaders, the government thus being made doubly illegal. The reasons for these acts included the distance of America from England and the desire of the leading colonists to govern themselves without interference from the home country.

With local variations the story of the colonial struggle for administrative (rather than political) independence explains much of our later legal history. Speaking generally, we may say that the standard form of colonial governments came to be that of a governor appointed by the crown, of an upper house appointed by the governor or elected subject to his veto power, and a lower, popularly elected assembly. In some cases the upper house had judicial functions, and many judges, such as those in the admiralty courts, were appointed by the Crown. The colonists were settled on the edge of a vastly rich, virgin continent which fairly cried aloud to be profitably exploited. Imperial legislation was considered to be, and frequently was, a hampering influence. In this complex we may find the beginning of the disease of lawlessness.

Law must have some sanction. There can be only three. It may be considered either as the dictum of some supernatural being, or as the command of an earthly sovereign,—not, of course, necessarily an individual,—or as receiving its sanctity from the consent of the governed. The supernatural was tried only in New England theocracies, and soon abandoned as unworkable. The sovereignty of the empire obviously resided in "the King in Parliament," but that, for practical purposes, the colonists usually denied or strove against. The consent of the governed, in a strictly local sense, was all that remained, and it has continued, also in a local or partial sense, to control American obedience to law. Even if local law was fairly well obeyed when passed by the colonists themselves, respect for law as law could not fail to be lessened by their constant breaking or ignoring of the imperial laws. Without attempting to go into detail or to adopt a chronological arrangement, we may note some of the ways in which this was brought about.

A constant source of lawbreaking, particularly in the North, was the legislation by Parliament with regard to what were called "the King's Woods." In that day of sailing ships, trees suitable for masts were in great demand. England preferred to depend upon the forests of America rather than upon the foreign ones of the Baltic Provinces, and laws were made to save for the use of the Royal Navy all trees above a certain size upon lands not specifically granted to individuals. The colonists on the spot felt this to be an abridgement of their right to exploit the continent and use all its resources themselves. Not only were the laws disobeyed and the authority of the officially and legally appointed "Surveyors of the Woods" flouted, but force was used to oppose authority, and rioting not seldom was employed against law.

Again, according to the generally accepted economic theory of the day, colonists were supposed not to manufacture in competition with the home country, but to supply her with the raw materials. Laws against manufacturing worked, as a rule, but little hardship on the colonies, owing to high wages, scarcity of skilled labor, and other reasons, but they did in a few instances, as in the case of wool and smaller hardware such as nails. These were mostly household manufactures, but they were carried on by nearly every household in conscious defiance of imperial laws.

After the French and Indian War and the acquisition from France of Canada and the West, the British Government by proclamation in 1763 forbade any settlement in the new regions, the intent being to consider the problem deliberately in the light of Indian and other relations which the colonists had never been able to agree upon among themselves. Owing to procrastination, this temporary, and to the colonists most galling, restriction was not removed. Settlers and traders ignored the proclamation and poured into the new territory, all against the law. In fact, whenever there was profit to be made, the colonists ignored even their own laws. Most colonists had legislated against selling firearms or spirits to the Indians because of the obvious dangers involved, but these laws were constantly transgressed. In New York it was made illegal to trade with the French in Canada by way of Albany because by so doing the French were enabled to strengthen their Indian alliances at the expense of the colonists, but the temptation to profit was too great, and the merchants not only broke the law, but plotted to secure the removal of the governor whose farsighted policy had insisted upon its passage.

Of even more pernicious effect were the laws of trade. For example, in 1733, owing to the insistence of the West Indian sugar planters, Parliament passed an act placing a prohibitive duty upon the importation into the continental colonies of any molasses from foreign islands. The problem was a triangular one and no attempted solution of it could be fair to all three parties involved. For reasons which we need not go into, had this law been obeyed, the commerce of New England, including its profitable slave trade, would have been ruined. The law was never obeyed, but as a consequence, the New Englanders became a race of smugglers, and the most reputable merchants became lawbreakers. In this case, smuggling and lawbreaking were forced upon them, but, having become used to them, they passed on to smuggling when there was no reason but increased profit. In the French and Indian War, twenty years later, we find the merchants trading with the enemy on a scale which certainly prolonged the war, and in the decade before the Revolution men like John Hancock did not hesitate to smuggle wines on which there was only a moderate duty, and even forcibly to resist the authorities in doing so. As the Revolution drew nearer, the radicals made it a point of patriotic duty to break the English laws, and force and mob violence became more and more common. The Boston Tea Party is a case in point. That wanton destruction of fifty thousand dollars' worth of private property was in no way essential to the patriotic cause and was condemned by many of the patriot party.

As a result of the imperial-colonial situation through a

century and a half, only some of the aspects of which we touched upon, there steadily developed a disrespect for law as law and a habit of lawbreaking. The colonists made up their minds not to obey law, but merely to obey such laws as they individually approved of or such as did not interfere with their own convenience or profit. We are not arguing the ethics or rights of the cases, but merely stating facts and results. Moreover, in every colony there was constant conflict with the royal governors, so that the executive power came to be considered as inherently something to be distrusted and limited as far as possible, a feeling which is strong today as an inheritance from our colonial past. The executive, represented to the colonists as a hostile and outside power in their "constitutions," came to appear a power to be disobeyed and thwarted whenever feasible. In a similar way did the judicial. The people stood together to defeat the courts and to protect friends and neighbors. This was particularly notable in the admiralty courts and all cases prosecuted under the laws of trade. Juries would not convict no matter how flagrant the smuggling or other lawbreaking. Thwarting courts and officials became as much a game on the part of otherwise reputable people as fooling prohibition officers to-day.

In the South another element was introduced into the complex situation by slavery. There were slaves in the North also, but for the most part in too small numbers to affect the matter greatly. In the South the large numbers of blacks, many of them recently imported from the jungle, and their peculiar status as personal property, resulted in legislation and judicial administration which tended to some extent to break down respect for law. In Maryland and

many other colonies, for example, a negro was not allowed
to testify against a white man. Moreover, the court in
which the slave was most likely to be tried was that pre-
sided over by a single local magistrate, a slave-owner himself.
In Virginia until 1732, if a master killed his slave in consequence of "lawful correction," it was viewed merely as "acci-
dental homicide." The raping of a female slave was "trespass
upon property"! If we consider the laws relating to the
negro, and the relations between him and the whites, even
admitting that the great majority of slave-owners may have
been kindly, it is evident that in the two centuries of the
existence of the institution among us an immense amount of
crime must have gone not only unpunished but without fear
of punishment.

One other element may be taken into consideration, the
effect of the frontier. Until thirty years ago, America has
always had a frontier, and that fact has been of prime importance in many respects for the national outlook. For our
purpose we may merely note that in the rough life of the
border there is scant recognition for law as law. Frequently
remote from the courts and authority of the established
communities left behind, the frontiersman not only has to
enforce his own law, but he elects what laws he shall enforce
and what he shall cease to observe. Payment of debt,
especially to the older settlements, may come to be looked
upon lightly, whereas horse stealing may be punishable with
shooting at sight.

III

When the colonies united and won their independence
and the United States was formed, there had thus already

developed a fairly definite attitude toward law and authority. In many respects, owing mainly to their economic prosperity, the colonies were more law-abiding than Europe. In all my research, for example, I have found only one case of a traveler being robbed on the highways. Moreover, the colonists came to be a kindly and hospitable folk, and crimes involving brutality were proportionately less common than in the Europe of that day or the United States of this. But the essential point is that Americans had developed a marked tendency to obey only such laws as they chose to obey, and a disregard of law as law. Laws which did not suit the people, or even certain classes, were disobeyed constantly, with impunity and without thought. A habit had grown up of attempting to thwart the courts and judges, of distrusting the executive, and of relying solely upon the legislatures. Juries had got into the way of not considering the law, but merely their own or their neighbor's interests. When cases became desperate or law officers made some show of real enforcement, as did occasionally a rare Surveyor of the Woods or a customhouse officer, they were taken care of by mobs, and as a rule the absence of any real force behind the show of royal authority made the officials powerless. In the national period we shall see the fruits of this long training in disrespect for law.

We need not linger over Shay's Rebellion in Massachusetts in 1787, when mobs of malcontents with genuine grievances forced the closing of courts and brought the state to the verge of civil war; or the Whiskey Insurrection in 1794 in Pennsylvania, when attempts to enforce an excise tax required the use of fifteen thousand Federal troops. Nor need we go into the practical nullification of Federal laws and

authority by some of the New England states in the War
of 1812, or the smuggling and trading with the enemy
during that ill-advised conflict; or into the threatened
nullification of the Federal tariff by South Carolina some
years later. The ripest fruits of disregard for law are found
mainly when passions are aroused, as they were for several
decades from 1830 onward. We will briefly touch first upon
the persecution of the Irish and Catholics, in which law and
order were abandoned from 1833 to 1853. The building of
the Baltimore Railroad was punctuated by race riots. Even
the militia failed to quell a similar one on the Chesapeake
and Ohio, and a "treaty" had to be drawn up. In 1834 the
Ursuline Convent near Boston was burned to the ground
and sacked by anti-Catholics. The next night a race riot,
this time directed against negroes, broke out in Philadelphia
in the course of which thirty houses were sacked or de-
stroyed, a church pulled down, and several persons killed.
Similar riots occurred within a few weeks at other places,
and in a few years the militia had to disperse a mob of two
thousand marching on the house of the Papal Nuncio at
Cincinnati. The Irish quarter in Chelsea, Massachusetts,
was attacked; the chapel at Coburg was burned, that at
Dorchester blown up, and that at Manchester, New Hamp-
shire, wrecked; at Ellsworth, Maine, the priest was tarred
and feathered; the convent at Providence was attacked;
and at St. Louis a riot resulted in ten deaths. But it is
unnecessary to detail more, such incidents being all too
common throughout the country.

Similar violence was used against the Mormons, mainly
while they were resident in Missouri and before they had
adopted the doctrine of plural wives. The feeling against

[111]

partially discarded for our purpose, though they probably would not have occurred in a country in which the people had an ingrained sense of law. The worst one in New York, in 1863, lasted four days and resulted in the destruction of $1,500,000 worth of property and the loss of one thousand killed and wounded. It was followed by lesser riots at Detroit, Kingston, Elmira, Newark, and elsewhere. In the country districts threats of arson and murder were openly made.

The war over, we found ourselves with the Fourteenth and Fifteenth Amendments to the Constitution, giving the negro the right of suffrage. However these may or may not have been observed in the North, it is obvious that they could not be and never have been in the South. To have observed these Amendments, particularly the Fifteenth, in some states, such as Alabama, where the negroes outnumbered the whites, meant that the whites might be ruled by the blacks, and in any case it meant serious trouble, racial feeling being what it was then and is now. The complete nullification of such laws, having all the sanction of being parts of the Constitution, could not fail to reduce respect for law. Again, Americans obeyed such laws as they chose, and disregarded or opposed by force such as they did not choose.

IV

We may now come to another phase of our national lawlessness. There is a good deal of popular misunderstanding with regard to lynching. It is generally regarded as rather peculiarly a Southern institution, and the consequence of

[114]

attempts at rape on whites by negroes. The term "lynch law" appears to have been first used in 1834, and it is from that time that the practice of lynching became common in the United States. At first the most notorious cases were those of gamblers, such as occurred in Vicksburg, Mississippi, and in Virginia. It was, however, also practised in the North, and spread to California and the West after the discovery of gold. In California, in 1855, out of five hundred and thirty-five homicides committed there were but seven legal executions. The celebrated Vigilance Committees were formed in San Francisco, each of which hanged four men and banished about thirty. These "popular tribunals" were also formed in Utah, Nevada, Oregon, Washington, Idaho, Montana, Arizona, New Mexico, and Colorado during their early periods of settlement.

That lynching was not confined to negroes, the South, or the crime of rape is easily proved by such statistics as we have. I have no recent figures, but as this chapter is concerned with our "heritage," and not our present lawlessness, this is not of account. In 1900 over 52 per cent of the persons lynched in Illinois were white, over 78 per cent in Indiana, over 54 per cent in Missouri, over 38 per cent in Kentucky, and over 35 per cent in Texas. Tables prepared by the United States Government failed to show any relation between the distribution of lynchings and the proportions of blacks to the total state populations. Nor did they show any correlation between the numbers of lynchings and the percentages of illiterates or foreigners. The responsibility therefore must rest on the literate native element.

In the period from 1882 to 1903 there were 2585 persons lynched in the Southern states, of whom 567 were whites,

1985 negroes, and 33 "others"; in the Western states the figures were, respectively, 523 whites, 34 negroes, and 75; in the Eastern states, 79 whites, 41 negroes, and no "others." In the country as a whole there were thus lynched in the twenty years 3337 persons, of whom 1169, or over one-third, were white, and 2060 negroes. In all three sections the crime for which the greatest number of lynchings occurred was murder. Rape comes next, with "minor offenses," arson, theft, assault, following in much smaller proportions. In our country in a time of perfect peace there were thus an average of between three and four lynchings every week in the year for the twenty-year period chosen by hazard for examination. Allowing for the difference of population, is it possible to conceive of two persons being murdered by individual citizens, instead of allowing justice to take its course, every week in England or France for a generation?

In the above rapid and wholly inadequate survey no attention has been paid to the problem or statistics of ordinary crime. The United States has no adequate criminal statistics even at the present day. Such a survey projected into the past would be impossible. I have not been concerned with, so to say, "crimes under law," but with opposition to or disrespect for law itself as law. Even thus I have neglected much which would properly be included in a full treatment of the subject.

It is needless to say that we are not going to be able to shed this heritage quickly or easily. In fact we have gone so far on the wrong road that it is by no means certain that we can ever get back on the right one even with the best of intentions. Inbred respect for law, as I said in the beginning, is a plant of slow growth. For three centuries we have been developing disrespect. Our heritage has made recovery more difficult for us by bringing about conditions that themselves help to increase our disrespect and lawlessness, aside from the feeling of the individual citizen. This portion of our heritage is in some part from our Puritan ancestry, North and South. The Puritans insisted that their own ideals of life and manners should be forced on the community at large, and they also believed that any desirable change could be brought about by legislation. Partly from Puritanism and partly from the exaggerated influence attributed to the legislatures in colonial days for the reasons I have noted above, Americans have believed that their ideals should be expressed in the form of law, regardless of the practical question of whether such laws could be enforced. They have apparently considered that the mere presence of such laws will help *respect* for the *ideal* of conduct, regardless of the fact that the presence of such unenforceable laws will bring about *disrespect for law itself*. Every minority which has had a bee in its bonnet has attempted to make that bee "home" into a law, and to a remarkable extent the majorities have not cared, partly because they take little interest in public affairs, but mainly because they imagine that even if some "fool law" is passed they can disobey it if they choose, as they have others. Because we have ceased to have any respect for law we allow any sort of laws to be passed, and then—the vicious circle continuing—our disrespect increases yet more because of the nature of such laws. When Americans talk about their glorious past, it may be well for them to remember that we have one of the most sinister inheritances in this matter of law from which any civilized nation could suffer, a heritage that we are apparently passing down to our children in a still worse form. For this reason, if for no other, I believe that the unenforced and unenforceable Eighteenth Amendment was one of the heaviest blows ever directed against the moral life of any nation.

CHAPTER VI

HOOVER AND LAW
OBSERVANCE

HOOVER AND LAW OBSERVANCE

I

To an American citizen profoundly interested in the welfare of his country, it is all too obvious that the one fundamental question transcending all others is that of law and the observance of law. Prosperity may temporarily increase or decline. The manufacturers may get the extra profits they desire from a prohibitive tariff or they may not. The farmers, like the intellectual classes, may for a time be out of adjustment with the earning power of other classes and the general economic level. America may for a while either accept or refuse its responsibilities to the world at large. But far more fundamental than these or any other problems confronting this country at the moment is the problem of whether the United States is to remain a civilized nation or come to be ranked with Kipling's "lesser breeds without the law." It is evident that the present situation, which would disgrace a savage tribe, cannot continue along its indicated curve without leading directly to a breakdown of government or to a dictatorship. To a considerable extent, indeed, the government has already broken down in one of its most essential duties—the protection of the persons and properties of its citizens; as is evidenced by private policemen, armed guards, and armored cars, the citizens have had to undertake such protection for themselves.

So far as I know, Mr. Coolidge, intent on paring budgets,

never troubled himself over the rising tide of crime and lawlessness, beyond seeing to it that Mrs. Coolidge was accompanied on her shopping by an armed protector. It is therefore a matter of the most earnest congratulation that, although Mrs. Hoover has dispensed with a personal guard, Mr. Hoover is evidently sufficiently impressed by the situation to have devoted one-quarter of his inaugural address to the topic. A careful and sympathetic reading of that address, however, leaves one wondering whether he has the slightest comprehension of the magnitude and causes of the danger which we face, although a later public utterance shows some advance. In his Inaugural he said, indeed, that "the most malign of all these dangers [to the state] to-day is disregard and disobedience of law," and every honest citizen must whole-heartedly agree with him when he goes on to say that "our whole system of self-government will crumble either if officials elect what laws they will enforce or citizens elect what laws they will support. The worst evil of disregard for some law is that it destroys respect for all law."

But what remedy does he suggest, beyond appointing the inevitable investigating committee which, according to the custom of such bodies, will probably sit for from one to five years, publish a voluminous report, with perhaps one or two dissenting reports, and be discharged with thanks? The only recommendation he can offer is to say that "if citizens do not like a law, their duty as honest men and women is to discourage its violation; their right is openly to work for its repeal."

Obviously, from the context in which these passages are found, Mr. Hoover was thinking mainly of the Eighteenth Amendment, but as he rightly points out, and as we cannot too strongly stress, the whole observance of law hangs together. A loose administration which would allow officials to pick and choose among the laws they enforce, or citizens to determine at will which laws they obey, could only be destructive of any real sense of law on the part of the public. The American problem, though complicated by Prohibition, lies far deeper; and it is the lack of understanding as to what the problem is that so greatly diminishes the force of Mr. Hoover's appeal to us as citizens anxious to do our duty toward society.

II

It is needless to waste words in painting the situation in our country to-day. The headlines of any metropolitan newspaper any day do so only too clearly. Crime of the most desperate sort is so rampant that unless a robbery runs into six figures or a murder is outstandingly brutal or intriguing, we no longer even read below the headings. We are no more interested than in a stock that does not move. We have ceased to expect criminals to be caught and punished. We accept the statement from the Chief Justice of the United States that our criminal justice is a disgrace to civilization with the same lack of reaction with which we accept the Department of Agriculture's estimate of the cotton crop as about the same as was expected. On the other hand, tens of thousands of reputable citizens, who in all the private relations of life are decent and trustworthy persons, are daily breaking one law or another. When a state has ceased to be able to enforce law, when its citizens have ceased to feel any sense of duty to obey law as law, when they have lost all respect for law as law, when they have lost all respect for law enforcement and the courts and officials charged with enforcement, it is clear that something more than merely one amendment to the Constitution, however unwise, must be sought for as the cause.

With regard to the increase of crime of one type and the failure of the American state to protect its citizens, I can from personal experiences date a marked change with some accuracy. I was in Wall Street in business until about 1912. From about 1900 to that date I was usually the one in my office, first as manager and then as partner, who saw daily to getting the securities from the safe deposit vault to the office in the morning and back again at night. The value of the negotiable securities and cash sometimes ran to a couple of millions. Unarmed and unguarded, with only an office boy to carry the boxes, it never once occurred to me or to anyone else in that period that there was any danger to the securities or to myself in so carrying them through the public streets. About 1908 or 1909, I think it was, New York State passed a new law taxing the securities of non-resident decedents if the securities were in a New York safe deposit at the time of death. In order to avoid this extra taxation, a member of my family, a resident of New Jersey, decided to transfer his securities to Hoboken. I did it for him by the simple method of putting about two hundred thousand dollars, worth of coupon bonds in a suit case and carrying it, unguarded and, indeed, unaccompanied from Wall Street down to the old Hoboken Ferry, over the Ferry, through the streets of Hoboken, along the river front to the Trust Company in that city,—again without thought of risk or danger.

Let us note the difference today. Going abroad to stay for a considerable period, I decided last December (1928) to transfer my securities from bank vaults at practically the corner of Hanover and Wall Streets, to a bank which would keep them in custody for me, cutting coupons, and so on without trouble to me. I first thought of transferring them to an institution just over the river in Brooklyn. On asking the Vice-president how, in view of modern crime conditions, the actual physical transfer would be made, he answered as follows: "We have our own armored car, with three men in it. We are, of course, very careful in selecting them in the first place, but we always have a detective who keeps track of them. The chauffeur sits in front of the car, and behind him we have a guard who keeps his revolver in his hand so that if the chauffeur starts any tricks he has a gun in his neck at once. In the back of the car sits the third man, who keeps his foot on a valve which by pressure would shut off the supply of gas at once. If a fracas should start between the other two, he would stop the car. If you would care to do so, you could also come in the car with your securities." I decided finally on a trust company in Wall Street, very near the vault where the securities were, and where I would have to walk only a block. There it was agreed that two armed guards would meet me when I was ready to make the transfer. One day, with my wife and sister, who also had securities, I went to the vault. In my innocence I suggested that I would telephone to the trust company to send over the guards. The official at the vault hesitated, and then said: "If I were you I would go to the trust company and get them, so as to be sure that no one is listening in, and that the men who come are really the men sent by the company."

I spent half my waking hours in one state and half in the other, and I lived under two different sets of laws relating to inheritance, taxation, and to innumerable other matters of daily concern. Had I commuted to Connecticut instead of to New Jersey, I should have had to learn an entirely new set of laws and regulations, for ignorance of the law is no excuse for disobedience.

This anomalous condition is found throughout the country; in countless minor matters it is impossible to tell whether one is obeying the law or not. Motoring from New London to Providence, one must not run at *more* than thirty miles an hour, I believe it is, if there is now any speed limit, in Connecticut; but as soon as one has crossed into Rhode Island it is against the law to run at *less* than thirty. Traveling on the train from Buffalo to Chicago, it is legal to buy cigarettes for the first hour or two; but after crossing into Ohio (no one knows when or where) it becomes illegal for two or three hours until one has again reached the safety of Indiana. Before Prohibition, it used to be legal for one to have a flask of whisky while going by train from Denver to Dallas—up to the imaginary line which separated some county in Texas from another, at which point one was a lawbreaker, and, as occasionally happened, could be hauled from the train and jailed. Ignorance of the law, as we have said, is considered to be no excuse. A law-abiding citizen who finds himself frequently breaking such laws feels none of the emotions which a reputable citizen should feel in such circumstances, and the fact that the situation is so obviously absurd insidiously breaks down the feeling that law as law should be implicitly obeyed.

Again, many laws are passed merely because it is the easiest way for lazy or supine legislators to rid themselves of noisy and fanatical minorities; likewise they may be passed by legislators who are simply ignorant or have some racial ax to grind. As instances we may cite the law prohibiting the teaching of evolution in Tennessee; the law recently passed by one of the Southern states, prohibiting the presence in any public or school library of any book "defining evolution" (which would rule out all dictionaries and encyclopedias); or the several so-called "pure history laws," penalizing the critical writing of American history. Included also in this group are the broad censorship laws of various places, such as that which in St. Louis resulted in the seizure and destruction of a collector's rare edition of Boccaccio, and that which makes it illegal for bookstores in Boston to sell a considerable number of current volumes sold almost everywhere else in the United States. As I write these lines my attention is called to the latest limitation of my liberty. I have in my library here that finest of all war books, *All Quiet on the Western Front.* The author comes nearer to telling the truth, the whole horrible stench of truth, about war than has anyone else. War is brutal, and it would be well if people could know how brutal. One or two incidents are brutally told, but there is nothing pornographic in the whole book. Yet I discover it can be published in America only in an expurgated form and that if I take my copy home it will be confiscated. My government will not allow me to read what any European in any country is free to do, and I am faced by the dilemma of either having to destroy or give away a fine book which I have bought here quite legally and with entire honesty of mind, or having to break the law of my native land and smuggle it in.

In constantly passing back and forth from Europe, I am continually confronted by similar problems. In all enlightened countries over here not only are treatises on birth control by medical authorities to be had in the bookshops of any city, but frequently public instruction is given in free clinics. If I take any such book home to New York, I become a lawbreaker and am liable, I believe, to a year in prison or five thousand dollars' fine. I am interested in modern literature and, although greatly disliking the book, I realize that Joyce's *Ulysses* is a landmark in its development. For the purposes of an article I am now writing I can readily buy *Ulysses* for five dollars in Paris or here in London (where I am working at the moment), but if I take it to New York to use there, I shall again be a lawbreaker and shall again be liable to a year in prison or five thousand dollars' fine.

Recently the Federal authorities in Boston ruled that it was illegal to import copies of that classic, Voltaire's *Candide*, which is required reading for the students at Harvard, Radcliffe and, I believe, Wellesley. The boys and girls are thus faced at the outset of their careers as citizens with the delightful dilemma as to which they will obey, the Harvard and Radcliffe authorities or the Customs Officers clothed with Federal authority. If they do not buy the book they are refusing to do required college work; if they do, they are breaking the Customs laws. Thus early does a paternal government gently lead youth on the path of lawbreaking and laughing disrespect for law. Living under laws like these, is it any wonder that the sober, law-abiding citizen has little respect for law as law?

III

But let us consider such a citizen facing some concrete problems. Personally I agree heartily with all that Mr. Hoover says. I have keen respect for law and believe that such a respect is an essential element in building up any civilization. But what is the situation in America that confronts such a normal, law-abiding citizen? Is a citizen of Boston who wishes to know what is being written in contemporary American literature bound to deprive himself of knowing anything about a dozen or so important titles because it is illegal for a bookseller to furnish him with them? Or shall he surreptitiously import them from New York, or break the law and buy them furtively from a "book-legger"? Shall a teacher in the state which prohibits dictionaries and encyclopedias in its schools and libraries throw those books out of the windows, or shall he give the students illegal use of copies hid in closets? Shall a man interested in Italian literature and the culture of the Renaissance leave a hole in his knowledge where Boccaccio should be, or shall he break the law and buy a copy? Shall I destroy the books which I buy in Europe or take them home? Shall the Harvard students read *Candide* or obey the law and flunk their work?

Consider the question of possessing firearms in New York State. Any thug can readily procure a revolver by the simple process of going across the river to New Jersey and buying one; but it has become increasingly difficult and in many instances impossible for the law-abiding citizen who wishes to protect his home from the thug to get a permit. The Constitution of the United States says that the right of the citizen to bear arms shall not be abridged, but this has been abrogated by the "police power" of the states, so that we now have a situation in which any thug can get a gun, but the sober citizen often cannot. In fact, in a recent skirmish in New York which resulted in the killing of a policeman by thugs, it was found that the officer was acting as "gun-toter" for a rival gang of thugs who had no desire to be caught with the tools of their trade—three guns—on their persons. Some years ago a concern with which I had relations had its pay roll of about five thousand dollars brought to the factory through a bad neighborhood every Saturday by a trusted employee. (This was before the breakdown in government had become so complete as to make it profitable for private companies owning armored cars to perform that service for business men.) Since there had been many holdups, the company attempted, unsuccessfully, to get a permit for the messenger to carry a revolver. After a while it was discovered that the difficulty lay in omitting to tender the usual fifteen-dollar bribe to the police captain of the precinct. There was no use in carrying the matter higher. The company could not prefer charges, for in such situations there is never any proof. It had three options: to risk its five thousand and its employee's life by leaving him undefended; to break the law by bribing a police official; or to break it by having the messenger carry a gun without a license.

Recently one of my friends, driving a motor car in a large American city, was overhauled by a motorcycle policeman who told him, with foul language, that he had been speeding. As a matter of fact this accusation was not true, but it was the habit of this particular policeman to allow a car to get ahead and then, by speeding after, to show a high rate on his own speedometer. My friend would have had no case had he gone to court and, what he minded more than a possible fine, a black mark would have gone against his driver's license. Knowing the situation, he immediately placed his hand on his wallet pocket. "Mind you," said the policeman, "I'm not asking for anything." "All right," said my friend, handing him ten dollars. The cop smiled and speeded off to wait for his next victim and bill. It must have been a profitable business. Another friend of mine in a large contracting firm operating in a certain large city tells me that to their bids for every sizeable job they add, as do their competitors, an item of five hundred dollars. This is for the policeman on the beat, about fifty dollars a week being handed to him so that he shall not be constantly bothering them with unjustified complaints about obstructing the sidewalk by their operations. If the money is not paid, an official of the company has constantly to waste his time appearing in the police court to answer summonses. It is easy to say that, instead of breaking the law by bribing officers, my friends should have reported them. All I can say in reply to any enterprising private citizen is: let him try single-handed to clean up the police department of any large American city and see how far he will get.

Let us take another example. Let us suppose a person has some pre-Prohibition brandy in his house. Such possession is quite legal; but his father, living across the street, has a sudden heart attack and the family telephones over for the brandy. If the man takes it over, under the last law passed by Congress on the subject, he becomes a felon and is liable to ten thousand dollars' fine or five years in prison—or both. Should he leave his father to die while waiting for the law

[133]

to be repealed, or should he become a felon in the eyes of the law? For the reasons noted above, we have ceased to have much respect for ordinary laws; and now, under the teaching of Congress, we are likely to have no fear of even felony. The effect is subtle. Heretofore no self-respecting man could have borne to think of himself as genuinely a legal felon, for this term was applied only to those who committed arson, rape, homicide, and similar crimes. But no man is going to think that by breaking the Eighteenth Amendment he places himself in that category, although the law declares that such is his classification. The result will be to make the word "felon" lose its damning character.

IV

When laws are just and wise, they ought to be obeyed and are likely to be; but when they are not, they open very genuine problems in ethics for the decent citizen. I wonder if Mr. Hoover himself, with his love of efficiency, his sense of organization and efficient government, to say nothing of his racial pride, would under all circumstances insist upon an absolute observance of the Fifteenth Amendment? Should the negro race largely outnumber the white in any state (in Mississippi there are already 935,000 negroes to 854,000 whites), would he insist upon a strict observance of that amendment, even if it resulted in a negro government permanently set up over the whites? The situation, being a local one, would hardly result in a nation-wide repeal of the constitutional amendment. If Mr. Hoover were a resident of the state, what would he do? Would he live under the negroes, would he move away, or would he disobey the law?

Many cannot move away, and even if they could, I doubt if Mr. Hoover would willingly abandon any considerable number of states to negro republics.

Prediction is dangerous work but I think there is one prediction not hard to make. That is, that our having so unthinkingly written unenforceable prohibition into the Constitution, and our then insisting upon the sanctity of that Constitution, is going to result in time in the awakened negroes' insisting upon the observance of the Fifteenth Amendment. If Prohibition is sacred and inviolable because it is a constitutional amendment, how about negro suffrage? There are already rumblings being heard, and in my opinion the fanatical wets have not only split our country into bitterly opposed factions and decreased respect for the Constitution, but they have, without giving the matter a thought, brought the crisis of racial hostility nearer to us than it could ever have been brought in any other way. The time is rapidly coming, if the Methodists and Baptists and W.C.T.U. and all the other Prohibition forces insist upon the sanctity of the Eighteenth Amendment, when the fifteen million negroes, fast growing in wealth, education and racial self-consciousness and assertiveness, will insist upon the sanctity of the Fifteenth.

But we may also ask Mr. Hoover about the Fourth Amendment, which the officials of his government are constantly violating, certainly in spirit. "The right of the people to be secure in their persons, houses, papers, and effects, against unwarrantable searches and seizures, shall not be violated, and no warrants shall issue, but upon probable cause, supported by oath or affirmation, and particularly describing the place to be searched, and the persons or things to be seized."

Yet, without warrant and without probable cause, the agents of Mr. Hoover's own government have stopped, seized, searched and even murdered citizen after citizen in yacht or motor car within the past few months. Let Mr. Hoover and Mr. Mellon talk of law enforcement to the shades of John Adams and James Otis! What is the law-abiding citizen to do when driving his car on a lonely road with his wife or children he is told to halt by an un-uniformed man? How is he to tell whether the man is a thug who will rob him if he stops, or a legal officer of the United States government acting unconstitutionally? If he stops, he may be robbed or worse; if he does not stop, the agents of the United States government, as they have done time after time lately, may ruthlessly murder him. This is not a hypothetical case. It is an actual situation that confronts every citizen who has a car or a boat, and which has already resulted in the slaying of many innocent and law-abiding persons. Their wrongs and deaths have been thundered from the halls of Congress, but the government calmly says it will uphold its agents.

Mr. Hoover speaks easily of the right of citizens who disapprove any law "openly to work for its repeal," but he must realize the inherent difficulty of this for unorganized individuals. In the first place, for some obscure reason in the American character, laws are rarely repealed; they are allowed simply to lapse in observance. It is far more difficult to get any legislature, including Congress, to take an interest and initiative in repealing a law than it is to enact one. Getting a law repealed may mean no less than educating an entire state, which may take a long time and which most certainly will require a large expenditure of money. In the

second place, many of the laws to which the law-abiding
citizen objects were originally passed either through ignorance
of the electorate and the legislature or through the influence
of an organized minority whose crusade was well supplied
with funds by some fanatic angel. It is notorious how
politically effective even a small minority may be if sufficiently active, well organized, and wealthy; and in most instances, the opposition—the people who feel oppressed by
some law passed by the efforts of a minority—are both
unorganized and without adequate funds. To overcome
these handicaps takes time—a long time.

To-day the power of the individual is largely lost. An
enormous amount of money is necessary to place any movement before the public, as may be proved by a glance at the
sums spent by the Republicans in the last campaign to elect
even Mr. Hoover. Let me illustrate by an example. For a
while I had an apartment overlooking the harbor in Brooklyn.
The view was superb, but I soon found, as all others do there,
that the place was rendered impossible by the clouds of oily,
black smoke blown into our windows from the tugs and
steamers in the river. Complaining of the situation, I was
asked why I did not start a movement to remove the nui-
sance, and take advantage of the law which makes burning
soft coal in the harbor an offense punishable by a five-
hundred dollar fine. The answer was obvious. I had to
earn my living, and heading such a crusade was a full-time
job. I should have had to abandon my work, organize a
publicity bureau, spend large sums on postage and stationery,
form committees, and so on through the whole usual business. The help to be derived from the city authorities was
well indicated from the fact that the Municipal Building

itself appeared to be, and I was told was, one of the worst offenders in the use of the illegal fuel! It is against the law in New York to drive a car with the muffler cut out, yet Sunday afternoons in my apartment were rendered hideous for an hour or two Sunday after Sunday by a car running at top speed up and down several blocks, passing under my windows. Apparently the crew were merely cooling themselves off in the hot weather, and enjoying the noise and speed. Could I do anything? The car was part of the apparatus of the fire company a few blocks away. How far would I get in trying to enforce the municipal regulations against the municipality itself?

A friend of mine in another city, which passed an ordinance prohibiting the use of soft coal, spent several thousand dollars installing smoke-consuming apparatus in his plant. One day, sitting at his open window and being covered with soot from the three chimneys of an ice plant not far away, he decided to try his hand at law enforcement. He called up police headquarters and, after explaining the situation, received as answer, "You mind your damned business and we'll mind ours." The plant was owned by local politicians.

It is all right for Mr. Hoover to say obey the law or work for its repeal; but what is a tug-boat captain to do if all his competitors are saving money by burning soft coal, and if the government authorities not only do not enforce the law but break it themselves? Is he to abandon his business in order to organize an almost hopeless crusade to get the law changed or enforced, or is he to give up his business entirely? Is he to burn hard coal in competition with soft, or is he to break the law himself?

Time to organize committees, money to make their work

efficient—few people have either. And both are futile if the opposition is corrupt—and in power. No, Mr. Hoover, obeying the law until you can get it repealed is not so simple a way out in the America of to-day as your speech would imply.

The subject can take us even further. The theory of our government—that the majority shall rule—cannot safely be stretched too far. It broke down in 1860, and may again. Indeed, in several respects it is not even the theory. A very considerable part of the legislation under which the people of our country live and do business has, in the last resort, been the determination of a single judge of the Supreme Court passing upon the constitutionality of laws by votes of five to four. It was shown lately that owing to the method of repealing clauses in our Constitution, three million people strategically located in the right states could block the will of all the rest of the nation. In such a case would it be the duty of the nation to obey the law?

Theoretically there is no justice in the doctrine of majority rule. It is a useful and practical method of carrying on popular government, but that is all. No better method has been devised, but there is something abhorrent in the idea of fifty-one per cent of the population being able to force its ideas on forty-nine per cent—of sixty-one million people governing fifty-nine million. The fact is that it cannot be done without the acquiescence of the forty-nine per cent, or, indeed, any considerable minority. Fortunately the minority usually does acquiesce, for it realizes that the importance of carrying on the government is greater than any temporary discomfort or even oppression caused by the decision of the majority. But we must not lose sight of the

[139]

fact that in the American system sovereignty is supposed to reside in the people at large, and that majority rule is merely an expedient for determining the will of the people. But if the will of a sufficiently large minority is deliberately and persistently thwarted by the majority, revolt of some sort is inevitable.

V

In America revolt always takes one of two forms—nullification of the law or armed rebellion. We have had the American Revolution, Shay's Rebellion, the Whisky Insurrection, and the Civil War. The other method—nullification—has been used so often as to make it useless to catalogue even the more noted instances. No one believes for a moment that Prohibition will result in civil war; but it is obvious that this particular law is against the will of so large a minority, if it *is* a minority, of the people that thorough and impartial enforcement is impossible, and that the old American weapon of nullification will continue to be used against it. It is evident that not even the United States government can patrol eight thousand miles of boundary and put a policeman in every one of twenty million homes. A very considerable number of our people consider the law to be unwise, unjust, and tyrannical. Throughout the whole of English and American history there have always been men who had the courage to defy such laws, and, largely depending upon their ultimate success, history has recorded them as patriots or malefactors. I do not say that the Eighteenth Amendment is of such a character as to warrant infringement of it in the name of patriotism, but I do believe that is unwise and unjust, and it does seem to me to come perilously near being tyrannical.

Turning back again to the more general question, however, I cannot agree with Mr. Hoover that the solution of the lawlessness of America, with the peril that it brings to our form of government, lies in so simple a formula as "obey every law on the statute book or get it repealed." Criminals are not going to obey any laws that are not enforced, and the governments—federal, state, and municipal—have largely abandoned their duty of law enforcement. Last autumn the *New York Telegram* reported that "Chicago racketeers boast of 215 murders in two years without a single conviction." In London in six months, with more than twice the population, there were eighteen murders and every single murderer either paid the legal penalty promptly or committed suicide before he was caught. But even law-abiding citizens will not obey laws which are but partially and unjustly enforced. Our whole history has proved that. Would one-tenth of the merchants of New York pay duties on their goods if they knew that the other nine-tenths were allowed to import free? Year after year, on returning home, I have scrupulously listed all my purchases for the customs men on the dock, and, I will add, have usually been treated courteously by them. But what incentive is there to do so when, as last year, in the cabin before landing, one heard the names of twelve Irish and Hebrew gentlemen, otherwise never heard before, called out as having been given the freedom of the port? For two hours I had to keep my wife, who was ill, on the dock in sweltering heat while these friends of somebody in the Treasury Department had whirled off at once to their hotels or homes without paying a cent or having a key of their baggage turned. Does not that sort of thing, encountered at every turn in America in relation to governments, city, state and national, tend to make a good citizen feel rather like a conscientious idiot than like an upholder of the wise and honest laws of his country? Can respect for law continue when its daily enforcement is a matter of friendship and favoritism? No—nor will citizens obey, nor as juries enforce, laws with unjust penalties. How many juries under the Jones Act will find a man guilty of taking a drink if the penalty is the same as for homicide? Nor will citizens obey laws, such as the smoke ordinances, which the government itself breaks. Nor will they obey laws which they believe thoroughly unjust and infringing on personal liberty. If disobedience to just laws leads to anarchy, obedience to unjust laws leads to tyranny, as our forefathers well understood and implored us to remember.

No, Mr. Hoover's formula will not do. The task is far greater. We shall not develop obedience to law in America until we have educated both our electorate and our legislators to a knowledge of the nature of law, to the limits of laws, and to their effects; until we have educated them both to a tolerance and a practical wisdom in the art of governing; until we have cleaned the Augean stables of our public life of their accumulated filth, and the governments themselves—municipal, state, and federal—obey and impartially enforce the law; until public opinion and public prosecutors demand the punishment of millionaires and of highly placed officials in Washington with the same rigor as would be meted out to the ordinary criminal; until the ideal of quickly accumulated wealth, by any means whatever, is made subordinate to the ideal of private and public virtue.

If Mr. Hoover merely tells the American people to obey every absurd law, every unenforced law, every unequally and unjustly enforced law, every unenforceable law, that is now on the statute books of the nation and our forty-eight sovereign states, he will get nowhere. If, on the other hand, he will undertake to show the people what underlies their problem, and assume the leadership in a crusade to reform the very foundations of their life—the rotten foundations that are at the bottom of the problem of our lawlessness— then he will prove the leader for whom America waits, and patriotism and nobility may again rise above efficiency and wealth. By that path only can America regain respect for law and for herself. Nor is it a question only of respect. Far down the path which America is now treading, at the end of the vista, in the shadow of the future, but all too clearly visible to the eye of the historian, stands, biding his time, the sinister figure of the man on horseback, the dictator who inevitably "saves society" when social insubordination and disintegration have become intolerable, when order has given place to chaos. We must rule or be ruled. Cæsar, Cromwell, Napoleon, Mussolini—the line is long and the sequence inevitable. America can be saved, but it must be by regeneration, not by efficiency. May Mr. Hoover ponder the problem and face the issue!

CHAPTER VII
TO "BE" OR TO "DO"

TO "BE" OR TO "DO"

I

A recent writer in a privately printed volume on education begins with the sentence: "What is the matter with our schools?—Everything." I would not go quite as far as that in a blanket indictment of our educational system, but I must confess that to an outside but interested observer the system appears to be more and more hopelessly uncertain of where it is trying to go or what it is trying to do—a welter of "isms" in a sea of expense, without the slightest agreement as to basic aims.

In looking back, it is of course very easy to underrate the real influence of one's teachers. In the past couple of days I have happened to note both Gibbon's characterization of his Oxford days as the most unprofitable of his whole career, and Henry Adams's of his four years at Harvard as wasted. I have often, however, tried to estimate just what my education did for my own incomparably less powerful mind. I must have had in all, I think, about twelve or thirteen years, and as I look back on them I am impressed with the appalling waste of time and effort. I was naturally a bookish and studious boy. I began collecting my library when I could not have been more than ten or twelve, and was an eager student, yet I was taught Latin, German, and French, with the result that I never could read either of the first two without a dictionary. In conversation I never could speak more than a sentence of any of the three, and I have never known an American student who could—that is, merely as a result of his studying a language in school and college. Yet, at thirty-five, I taught myself in a few months more Persian than I had ever learned of Latin in several years' drudgery in boyhood. I remember, during the war, meeting on the street in Paris a young French lad of about twelve, of the better class, who stopped me and asked where he could get for his collection one of the insignia which I was wearing as an American officer. He spoke English fluently and, on my asking where he had learned it, he replied, somewhat surprised, "Why, at school." In America, with all the colossal expenditure on buildings, that is a feat which, so far as I know, no American school has ever accomplished for one of its pupils.

Of history as I may have been taught it, I can remember nothing. So far as I can now discern, all my historical knowledge, moderate as it is, has been acquired by reading, long years subsequent to the ending of my formal "education." That I do not remember facts from my years spent on "American," "Ancient," and "European" history may be due to a poor memory, but apparently history was taught merely *as* facts. The rudiments of spelling and mathematics have undoubtedly been useful. As far as my institutional education was concerned, the arts of painting, sculpture, architecture and music were simply nonexistent. I never heard a word about the world of delight to be found in them or of their possible influence on the life of the spirit. Of my struggles with grammar there remains nothing, not a single rule, so laboriously studied. I came of a cultured family and learned at home to use my mother tongue with a moderate degree of correctness. On the other hand, from my experience with country people in a village where I was on the Board of Education, I could not see that if they did not speak correctly by home training, they ever learned to do so in school. Of my physics and chemistry I have only hazy recollections. From mineralogy, geology, physiology, psychology, and zoology much less remained to me than from botany which I taught myself, learning, without forgetting, to name the trees and wildflowers and something of the general science.

I have always been greatly interested in philosophy, and I well recall with what anticipations I went from my small college to Yale to get what I thought would be a genuine initiation into the subject under the late Professor Ladd. Never were a student's hopes doomed to more swift and complete annihilation. As I recall it, in his course he lectured to over three hundred students. During the lectures some of his audience read novels, some newspapers, while a few "grinds" like myself ruined their handwriting trying to keep up with the lecturer in their note-taking. After another hour's work in my study rewriting the notes, I had a lecture written in longhand that was far inferior in exactness and proper expression to any chapter in a textbook that Ladd might have written, and after two hours' waste of time I had merely reached the point of having an imperfect text to study.

With the exception of one Japanese, none of the students whom I happened to know took the slightest interest in the subject. I had hoped that there might be opportunity, so essential in philosophy above all other studies, for some direct play of mind between my own uninstructed one and that of the instructor. There never was. The professor was a mere unapproachable oral textbook. Nevertheless, he had the illusion that studying "under him" *had* induced some play of mind among his novel-readers, and for that reason he used to give out the examination questions at the year's end so that the student might give original thought to them. Five of my friends were among the novel-readers. Having paid no attention to the course the entire year, they got me to sit under the apple trees at Ik Marvel's place, and for a couple of afternoons before the examination I talked over the questions with them. They all passed, with higher marks, I believe, than I did myself, and received Yale's *imprimatur* that they were proficient in philosophy.

Since I had completely lost the desire to teach which had taken me to the University, I took my Master's degree and let a Ph.D. go hang. I have never regretted the step, though I have no illusions as to the self-educated man's being as well trained as one who has had a genuine education. Thus ended mine, which had cost me a dozen years and my father certainly a minimum of six thousand dollars, pre-war. If it be objected that things are different to-day, I may add that I see no evidence of it; instead, I see an even greater confusion of aim and method. Not long ago I asked a well-known professor at one of the largest and best-known universities in the East what, in his candid opinion, his university did for the many thousands of students who annually attended it. After a moment's thought he said that as far as he could see, the university turned out a standardized, low-grade mental product, much like an intellectual Ford factory.

[150]

II

It is my experience that the professors themselves are getting thoroughly tired of the overorganization and intellectual aimlessness of our modern educational institutions. To a great extent they themselves are caught in the mill. I think that America is the only civilized country in the world where what a man *does* counts for so much more than what he *is*, and where the general public, having no cultural standard by which to judge what a man is, takes as the basis of appraisal solely the visible signs of what presumably he has "done." A college degree has come to have a perfectly absurd value in the eyes of the public, not only in regard to the graduates of an institution, but in connection with the teaching staff. It is practically impossible for a man who has not obtained his Ph.D. label to progress far in teaching as a profession. I cannot imagine any leading European university, such as Oxford, Cambridge or the Sorbonne, caring in the slightest whether a man who was otherwise qualified to teach within its halls had any degree at all, but every little picayune college or "university" of the fifteen hundred or more scattered over the United States has been seized with the Ph.D. mania. A member of the faculty of one of the oldest institutions in the country, who receives many requests from southern and western colleges for suitable men to teach on their staffs, told me that the one *sine qua non* on which they all insisted in their applications was that the candidate must have received his Doctor's degree. Otherwise, no matter how well educated, how brilliant intellectually, how good a teacher, the door was closed to him.

A year or two ago I was talking with a very successful

teacher of English literature in a prominent school for girls. She had only an A.B. but was soon, after many years' work, to have her sabbatical year. With sound instinct she wished to spend that year in England, becoming more familiar with the background of her subject, browsing as she wished among the masterpieces of the literature, and, at the end, bringing back to her pupils a wider knowledge, a deeper insight, and a freshened enthusiasm. But, no. She had reached the limit of salary to which she could ever attain with only an A.B., and therefore she felt it necessary to spend the year in the soul-killing routine of taking "English courses" at an American university to obtain an A.M. According to the American educational system, there was never a question of what she *was*, of what she could give to her pupils, of how, for their sake and her own, she could best spend that precious year outside the schoolroom, but of what tangible label she could wear, indicating to parents what she had "done". The pages of school and college catalogues listing the faculty must be scattered over with degrees, or the institution is suspect.

To a certain extent this might seem to be placing the responsibility on the public, but as is so often true in speaking of American education, we find ourselves arguing in a vicious circle. As Everett Dean Martin has well said, "The school cannot evade the responsibility for the present low level of mental life in this republic." Considering the enormous outlay for public education and the colossal sums represented by the endowments of our private institutions, we have a right to ask why, when educators have had resources undreamed of in any other land, they have created merely a muddled system and a general level of cultural attainment among our people below that of any one of eight or more European countries.

In so far as there appears to be any definite trend in American educational aims, it would seem to be toward President Eliot's ideal of "power and service"—one of the most baneful phrases, I fear, ever let loose by an educator upon an uneducated people. The stress is laid wholly upon the "doing." We have, more particularly in innumerable smaller colleges, courses in cost accounting, in real estate selling, in "business English," household decoration, basketball coaching as a profession, poultry raising, personnel management—all counting for "points" with philosophy or literature or science.

I cannot see that, as a general rule, American universities or colleges leave the slightest cultural impress upon those who attend them. Once out in the world, the ideals and the interests of most of the university men are identical with those of any "go-getter" who, since leaving high school, has been learning his trade of stockbroking or real estate selling or manufacturing in the world of experience. A man who has attended the Harvard Business School may indeed get ahead a bit faster than his less-tutored competitor, but that is because of his specific technical training, similar to that of a cabinetmaker or lawyer. Some corporations, after exhaustive research, have come to the conclusion that a "college man" is likely to prove more valuable in the competition of business than one who is not; but that may be explained on many grounds quite divorced from education. College men come from a class that is at least moderately well up in the economic scale, with all that this implies in producing a superior animal—good air, food, and the rest. Moreover, a college man has four years more of such things than has the non-college class. Then there are the social knowledge, the friendship, and the "mixing" experience gained in college. But none of these advantages is in any way related to the main business of a university in its undergraduate department, which is, to provide a cultural background and an education. The mere fact that the graduate is a better money-maker has nothing to do with that.

"For power and service." This phrase not only expresses a utilitarian view of education, but, in the true American spirit of haste, it has tended to emphasize the desire not only for "results"—that is, "practical" results—but immediate ones. It has emphasized our belief that "culture" either is something to help one in his economic career or else is a mere fandangle ornament for those who wish to "put on side"— not something vital in one's own spiritual growth. American education cannot be considered as disconnected from all the shortcuts advertised in almost every American journal—the fifteen-minute-a-day French courses that will enable you to entertain the representative of a foreign firm and in a week astonish your employer into raising your salary fifty per cent; or the scrapbook of the world's wisdom that will enable you to impress your hostess and to become popular in cultured society by a few moments a day; or the five-foot shelf that will make you the intellectual equal of the lifelong student. The American has no use for the old Greek saying that "good things are hard." He wants knowledge and wisdom without striving. His education has taught him no other path or ideal. If knowledge and culture are only for "power and service," why not buy them "canned," if it is possible, much as he stops at the service station to fill up with gas?

[154]

As compared with the "plants" of all our educational institutions in America, those of Europe make but a shabby showing for the most part—but they appear to get results that ours do not. There are idle students everywhere in all lands, but one cannot help comparing the mental outlook of the graduate of the high schools or "gymnasiums" or the universities abroad with those here at home and finding there a something which our students do not have—a maturity and a character.

The matter may be subjected to certain rough ways of measuring results as well. Leaving out such intellectual world centers as Paris, I may mention such a smaller town as Amsterdam, generally considered a mere minor trading and industrial center. In wandering about the streets of this northern Venice, one not only finds bookshops everywhere, but displayed in them the latest books, in four languages, on science, philosophy, and the arts. This fact speaks eloquently for the results attained by Dutch education of whatever sort it may be. There are plenty of cities in the United States of the same population—under seven hundred thousand—in which it would be difficult to get in even one language a tenth of the books offered at Amsterdam in four. Again, in the twenty-eight years that the Nobel Prize in literature has been offered, it has never yet been won by an American, though winners have come from practically every country in Europe and even from the Orient. Again, if we leave genius out of account and consider only the cultured public, we find that the number of books published in various countries in proportion to units of ten thousand inhabitants gives the following table:

Denmark............................. 11.4
Latvia.............................. 9.5
Holland............................. 9.0
Germany............................ 5.2
Norway............................. 4.7
France............................. 3.8
Great Britain....................... 3.0
United States....................... .85

Even such "backward" nations, according to our ideas, as Spain, Russia, and Poland produce more books in the above ratio than do we—the most abundantly supplied with money for education of all the nations in the world!

III

Our errors are fairly evident. For one thing, our democracy has harmed our education in two directions. On the one hand we have to a great extent turned over our public educational system to the people, although the weakest point in American life is perhaps its lack of public responsibility. Our city, and not seldom our state, politics are a byword and a hissing, a sink of corruption and ignorance; yet it is usually to them that we leave the selection of the membership in our Boards of Education. The cry is also raised that public money should be spent only in giving the public what it wants—and, in its uneducated and uncultured soul, what it wants is anything but a "liberal education." It all too often wants but two things: the ability to earn a better living; and the label of having been educated—a diploma or degree certifying that the recipient is as good as

any of the genuinely educated classes. As Lessing wrote a
century and a half ago:

> The iron pot longs to be lifted up
> By tongs of silver from the kitchen fire
> That it may think itself a silver urn.

This situation would be bad enough were it limited to the
public school and state university systems; but, as a competent critic has recently pointed out, too many of the
private colleges and universities have "gathered up their
academic gowns" and run after the mob "offering academic
standing to anything for which there is a popular demand."

Democracy, universal education, and high wages in the
laboring class have had another unfortunate influence upon
education by swamping our institutions with students who,
although some are admirable, have in all too many instances
no background at all, no desire to be really educated, and no
power of becoming so. For this reason there has been a
general movement during the past five years to simplify the
wording of textbooks in all the higher grades of school, and
even in our universities a professor has to choose his words
with great care. I am told that even at Harvard a professor
dare not speak of a king as having been "crowned," for fear
that the students will think he has been knocked on the
head! Thus a student coming from a home with cultural
background, with an intelligent mind, and a desire to learn,
has to be held back to a pace no faster than can be kept by
the son of an ironpuddler or a carpenter. This is no negligible point. As the Greeks said, "One comes to limp who
walks with the lame." The attempt to bring about mass
production in education has thrown enormous responsibility

upon, and created almost insoluble problems for, our educational leaders. A few generations ago the larger number of students in our higher educational institutions either came from well-to-do homes or else were boys of unusual gifts or ambitions. If a boy is really to receive the foundation of a liberal education by the time of his graduation from college, it is evident that what the college has to teach the boy who comes from one class of society is quite different from what it has to teach one from another. Education is far from being a mere matter of "book learning", though many are apt so to consider it. A person is far from being "educated" when his mind has merely been crammed with facts for four or even seven years.

Man is more than an intellectual machine, and a genuine education should develop and enable him to realize and utilize all sides of his nature. He is, for example, as much an æsthetic and an emotional creature as he is a reasoning one. Indeed, fundamentally he is more so. He reacted to emotion long before he began to reason, and developed art long before he did science, history, and all the rest of what now goes under the old term "book larnin'." In America, the emotional and æsthetic sides of man's nature, so deeply imbedded in it, are starved to an extent that they are almost nowhere in Europe. The great mass of our population, for example, rarely sees a really beautiful building. Compare the churches scattered all over the land with those which are the inheritance of the poorest in almost every community, however small, in England, France, Italy, Spain and other European countries. The great mass of our people, again, rarely see any genuine and beautiful sculpture. It is the same with painting. Not only are our greater museums poor in comparison with those of Europe but the distances are so great that the bulk of our people are hardly brought into contact at all with examples of really great art. In practically every country in Europe not only can some of the finest art be reached by almost anyone in a few hours' travel at most, but a man living almost anywhere can, in no more time than it takes to go from New York to Chicago, see all the greatest galleries, London, Paris, the Hague, Amsterdam, Vienna, Dresden, Florence, Rome, and the rest. In music it is much the same, although not to quite the same extent. America is practically a musical desert as compared with the life of ordinary people in Switzerland, Austria, Germany, or Denmark.

When the "privileged classes" are mentioned it is usually in an invidious sense, but there is a very real and inescapable way in which a boy brought up in a family which is cultured and which at least has money for travel *is* privileged as compared with the boy brought up in a home and a general environment that is not cultured and who has never seen anything beyond fifty miles from his village or small town until he goes to college. In the first case, a very large part of the boy's education has been carried on outside of college altogether. Social intercourse and foreign travel have given him certain elements of education utterly beyond the reach of the other. There is all the difference in the world, for example, between reading about the cathedral of Chartres and standing in it. In our emotional and æsthetic lives it is even more true than in other respects that we learn by experience. How are we really to educate the vast mob of boys and girls now crowding into our colleges, whose experience has been limited to the architecture of our Main Streets, learning the names of Beethoven and the other composers (or getting garbled versions of their works on radio or Victrola), and whose experience of great painting and sculpture is at most limited to black and white pictures in some book on art?

For the "privileged classes" college education in a way is supplementary education, but for a large part of those now crowding into the fifteen hundred colleges of America it is the whole of their education, and if it is limited to books, and, even worse, largely limited to what may be learned from books for the purely practical art of making a living, is it any wonder that the ideal and conception of "education" and "culture" are steadily narrowing? It must be remembered also that the college graduates of today will consider themselves the "educated" class of the future, and with the public largely in control of education, what will they consider education to be if they have been told they themselves were educated enough to get their degrees by studying chicken-raising with a little history and other things thrown in for the looks of it?

The self-educated person has all the handicaps of a first explorer in a new land. He may not always take the right roads. He does not see the country as a whole. He has to waste much time finding out things that everyone will know when the country has been well mapped. A genuine education should be of immense help in orienting us in the uncharted lands of the spirit. But that is just where so much current education fails us. It is merely a hodge-podge of miscellaneous and uncoördinated information that leaves the mind almost as bewildered at the end as at the beginning. Occasionally, indeed, given a strong mind, a self-educated person seems to have a better understanding of what education is than our educators. I have before me a remarkable letter from a workman, whose schooling stopped at the age of twelve. Being the eldest of a family of eight he then had to go into a factory, and though his position has much improved he is still in a factory, nor is he there in an executive job. From twelve to sixteen he put in ten hours a day of the most exhausting physical toil, but continued his studies in history by himself. From history he proceeded to philosophy, and the sciences of psychology, biology, physiology and physics. In translations he has read such French authors as Rabelais, Villon, France, Barbusse, Rolland, Proust, etc. Later he developed a taste for poetry, apparently becoming interested first through Keats and Tagore. Of music, he writes me: "I am fairly well acquainted with the best music, having attended symphonies, concerts and organ recitals since I was eighteen or nineteeen years old. I used to take what little money I had left after paying my board and go off to Pittsburgh alone to hear the New York, Philadelphia or Chicago orchestras perform. My taste for music was not created by the modern radio concerts. I acquired it from seeing and hearing Paur, Herbert, Stock, Damrosch, Muck and others." Much of his recent reading has been in Bosanquet, Alexander, Eddington, Whitehead and Bertrand Russell. He does not own a car but spends his holiday time hiking and studying nature as far from cars as he can get. He is bringing up his children and trying to instil into them the idea that education is much more than learning how to get a living; and incidentally he says he has found some of the secrets of a contented life.

I admit that here we have a very unusual case, but is it

too much to ask of an educational system which, at vast expense, takes a child at four or five and now carries him on to twenty or so, that it should succeed in doing for the student a little something of what this man has done for himself? What, among other things, has he taught himself? The joys of exact knowledge in science, of speculation in philosophy, the joys of nature, of music, of rational recreation and sane expenditure, and "some of the secrets of a contented life." How many American colleges of today would have given him as rounded an education as that?

Let us read another letter that is on my table. It is from a woman in one of the largest, wealthiest and most populated states in the Union, the public school system in which should be of the best. She began as a school teacher herself. "No doubt I did the work badly enough," she modestly writes, "but I did like to work with children and I began to study them. Then and there I became a rebel against the methods and system advocated and I departed from them just as much as I dared. After five years of teaching I married. Ten years ago my little daughter was born. Here was my opportunity to do as I pleased, for a while at least. I began by interesting her, talking to her as if she had a mind when she was a tiny baby. Before she was six months old, she had spoken several words plainly enough to be understood by disinterested persons. At thirteen months she was making sentences. Before she was three years old she was reading script and print. The most delightful books I could find were procured for her. Of her own volition she was learning much each day. She had no lessons. In her little *Readers* she began anywhere her fancy dictated. An eighth grade geography was worn out and another was procured. She browsed among the books we owned; at four reading from Holmes and Longfellow. At five she had read Poe and Hawthorne. At six years old I found her reading Emerson's essay on the Intellect. She had nature books and travel books, and we thought she was doing splendidly at home but to conform to custom at "half past six" we sent her to school (rural). She didn't fit anywhere. She was more interested in the work the eighth grade pupils were doing than that of the lower grades. Fortunately she had a tactful teacher. He did the best he could with her, finally placing her in fourth grade." The next year, under a teacher unfitted for her work, the child lost all interest. The following year she was kept home, "doing most excellent work". The next year she returned to school and for seventh grade work was given reading, spelling, grammar, arithmetic, penmanship, geography, local state history, United States history, physiology and health education. "At the end of the term the County Superintendent gives a final examination. Beginning at 8 o'clock the children write on all these subjects and also on Reading Circle books. They have till five o'clock to finish. . . . The County Superintendent gives the teachers the hint that final questions will be based on questions sent out through the term, so the teachers attempt to get the children to memorize the answers to these questions. There is a good cram before the examination. Of course most of them pass." The mother now faces the dilemma of continuing the ten year old child in school where she loses her interest and desire to learn, or teaching her at home which means that she will not have that shibboleth, a diploma, essential economically for almost any sort of job.

Here again, we may say, is an exceptional case, but it illustrates one of the most serious defects in our general education. That is that the educational system from bottom to top is coming to be operated more and more for the benefit of the unintelligent and not the intelligent. An educational system that is operated with public money should be run, so the easy logic runs, for the benefit of the public, all the public. Of course, the more of the public that enters the schools, the lower the work of the schools must be. Here and there there may be in a poor home an exceptionally keen and alert childish mind. Here and there is a poor home in which the parents are intelligent and do all possible to develop the child's mind and provide it with a stimulating mental environment. But we know these are exceptional cases and not the rule. With the lowered quality of teachers themselves, due to over-demand owing to mass classes, and with the teaching geared lower and lower to meet the requirements of a lower standard of pupil, from kindergarten to college, is not the chance for the really intelligent child getting less and less? How can an intelligent child from a home where intelligent and ambitious and mentally alive parents help to kindle all the child's interests and tastes be expected to take any interest in class work which is keyed to the rate of progress and general capacity of dull-witted children from homes that are cultural vacuums?

In many lines of private business and, I believe, in all government positions, a high school diploma is now essential. It has thus come to have an economic value, which has operated on education in two ways. It sends an enormous number of educationally unfit through the mill, not because they want an education but because they want the certificate

that admits them to a job. If they could buy one for ten
dollars they would much prefer to do so. This degrades
the ideal of education in the minds of pupils and teachers
alike, by making it serve primarily an economic and not a
humane end; and it hampers the education of the intelligent
pupil by dragging him down to the level of the vastly more
numerous unintelligent. Democracy considers it undemo-
cratic to spend public money on the few. It must be spent on
the many, but the many are not the equals of the few, and
there is no escaping the conclusion that our public educational system as we have it now, throughout every grade,
must sacrifice the intelligent, fit few to the supposed advantage of the heavy-minded, unfit many. I do not speak of the
few and the many in any snobbish sense. It is reasonable to
admit that a child brought up in a stimulating home environment, with all the advantages that a background of culture
and experience in its parents, and perhaps grandparents,
implies, meeting interesting people, hearing interesting
things discussed, and with other "privileges," is more apt
to be fit than one brought up in a dull, commonplace home
with none of these advantages. It is also reasonable to
admit that the number of homes of the first type are few and
of the latter, many. It is in that sense that I use the words
few and many.

Our great democracy claims to base its future upon education. On that, its spokesmen tell us, it must stand or fall;
but, we ask, what sort of education? Is it to be one aimed
chiefly at getting ahead in the world, at getting a white-
collar job instead of a manual one, an executive instead of
a clerical one, and so on? Or is it to be an education that
shall teach us, whatever our economic rank and position,

but the picture of the student body is all too true to life in such places. "The ambition of the 'co-eds' was to teach in a small town high school, not unlike the one where they had been educated. The town often hadn't even a library. Such girls couldn't waste their time developing a critical spirit. It would be suicidal for them if they did. Their happiest fate was to marry the town dentist or doctor, the clerk in the bank, the owner of the garage. Their highest ambition in life would be to send their children to Chippewa. The men in the College of Arts were generally serving time, taking the prerequisites to get them into the professional schools, or lazy boys content to loaf for four years before they settled down into business." As to the college life, the cheap toggery shops with the "cheap sport" clothes, the yet cheaper movies with student cat-calls at risqué incidents, the college "activities," do we not know them all too well as Miss Neff portrays them? Does this sort of thing, which is common enough all over the United States, go to make that "center of robust intellectual life" that Dr. Angell offers as the only alternative to "the life of the upper classes, whatever that may mean in America"? No, the choice is not between the "children of the upper classes" on the one hand, and "all those who possess qualifications of mind and character" on the other, but between those of all classes who have the desire and capacity for genuine education and those, again, of all classes who desire merely the social or economic benefit to be derived from the possession of a college diploma. If, as he says, the effort to answer his questions "will doubtless keep the educational pendulum swinging vigorously for many a day to come," all I can say is that the heads of our educational leaders are more bemused than even I have ever claimed them to be.

There are obviously two educations. One should teach us how to make a living, and the other how to live. Surely these should never be confused in the mind of any man who has the slightest inkling of what culture is. For most of us it is essential that we should make a living. In the old days we learned how to do it mainly in the shop or on the farm or by practice in the office of merchant, lawyer, or doctor. In the complications of modern life and with our increased accumulation of knowledge, it doubtless helps greatly to compress some years of experience into far fewer years by studying for a particular trade or profession in an institution; but that fact should not blind us to another—namely, that in so doing we are learning a trade or a profession, but are not getting a liberal education as human beings. It is merely learning how to make a living. Culture is essential in order to enable us to know how to live and how to get the best out of living, and a liberal education should help us on our way to acquire it, albeit the acquisition is a lifelong process. "Culture" is a much misused word and has come to have a very feminine and anæmic connotation in America. There have been innumerable definitions, but we may quote one of Matthew Arnold's as being as suggestive as any for our purpose. He speaks of culture as "a harmonious expansion of all the powers which make the beauty and worth of human nature." This is far removed from giving the degree of Bachelor of Arts to a student who has learned how to truss and dress poultry or has compassed the mysteries of how to sell real estate and run an apartment house.

Of course, life is short and getting rich is long—or may be.

Many people who go to college to-day, aside from their lack of *desire* for education, have no *time* for it, because it does not lead immediately to "power and service." This, to be sure, is nothing new. What *is* new is that a large proportion of the colleges have opened their arms to all such and have deceived them into believing that when they have gotten an olla-podrida of ill-digested information of a scientific and cultural sort, with the practical courses to teach them how to earn a better living more quickly, they have acquired a liberal education and are entitled to consider themselves Bachelors or Masters of Arts. The words, indeed, have come to signify as little as "gentleman" or "lady."

It all comes back, like most things, to the question of values—of what is worth while, of what is the good life. Should we learn French in order to impress the boss? Should we pick up scraps from collections of the classics in order to make a hit at Mrs. Jones's party and impress her guests? One of the most sympathetic of foreign critics and observers of American life, a man who has spent much time among us, recently said that one feeling he always had here was that all our goods were in our shop windows and there was nothing behind. I believe this criticism is all too true. We are so busy *doing* that we have no time to *be*. We all have almost forgotten what it is to *be*. We all have motor cars but no place to go. At present what we need above all else in America is education—not the infinitely variegated supply of courses that make a college catalogue look like Sears, Roebuck's, but a liberal education that will enable us to create a scale of values for our experiences and to take a philosophical attitude toward the complex reality about us.

If it be complained that most people have no time for an education that does not give immediate results, I again reply that that is their misfortune and has nothing to do with the matter. It is extremely unfortunate, if they are really capable of being educated, that they have no time for it; but, that being so, why tell them they *are* educated? Why not face the problem frankly and divide education (and degrees) into the two sections that I have suggested, the one to teach people how to make a living and the other to give them a *liberal* education, to teach them how to live, how to develop all those powers within themselves that make for the beauty and worth of life? If everyone in a democracy cannot have such an education (and a degree), neither can everyone have some of the other good things—a million dollars, or the talent that makes him a poet or painter or president of an advertising company.

IV

Is it not time that we stopped marking down all our spiritual goods to the price that the lowest in the cultural scale can pay? In the seventeenth century the lower middle class in Holland became very prosperous and there was a great demand for small paintings to adorn their new houses. As one of the historians of their art writes, instead of improving the quality of the art, this situation brought about a deterioration, because of the simple rule that "a large uneducated demand in any field can never produce anything but a glut of inferior commodity."

Whether a democracy can last is problematic, but it is certain it cannot last if there are no leaders above the general level. How are we to train them? Is it by training men solely for a particular calling—medicine, engineering, running a locomotive, or laundering collars? Or are we to give, to some at least, an education in which doing is subordinated to being, in which the development of intelligence and character shall be held superior to passing an examination in philosophy after reading novels for nine months, or learning how to truss and dress poultry? Sir Arthur Keith recently said, speaking of English education, that "it is self-discipline; the formation of character in making man's higher centers masters of his cerebral establishments." However it may be brought about—and that is something for the educators to decide (though they seem woefully at sea about it)—what the leaders of our civilization need in education is to be taught to *be* something, rather than merely how to *do* something.

In America, if I may repeat, far more than in Europe, the soul of the people depends upon the culture to be obtained by a genuinely liberal education. In Europe, in a sense, culture lies about one, for, in another definition of Arnold's, it is "contact with the best that has been thought and said." I happen to be writing this before my fire in London. Any errand that takes me into the streets—a visit to my agent in Fleet Street, a trip down into the City, a stroll through Whitehall—stirs more historical questions than a month in college could answer. Three minutes in one direction will take me to the marvelous collection of the Dutch masters gathered here for the time being from all the world. Ten minutes in a bus and I have the wonders of the Elgin marbles and the choicest sculpture of Greece for the asking. I am planning an ordinary week-end trip which in a few hours will take me to France or Holland, where entirely new sets of impressions and questions of every sort—æsthetic, historic, racial—will be aroused in spite of myself.

It is far easier here, as I well know from years spent on both sides of the world, to stress *being* instead of *doing* than it is in any corner of my native land. In America not only is it almost impossible to get into contact with "the best that has been said and thought," save through books alone, but *doing* has been exalted into a national cult and *being* is despised by public opinion as something enervating and almost disgraceful for a man to consider, something tainted with the idea of "idleness-and-leisure," which are usually hyphenated in America.

"Power and service." But of what earthly use is power unless it is to produce or secure something worth while, and of what use is service unless it is to serve some desirable end? In so far as any ideal is considered an end in America, it is the ideal of "a better life for everyone of every class"; but that merely puts off the question one stage further. What is a better life? Are not power and service merely *means*, just as are dynamos or locomotives? And what can the end be except a state of *being* desirable to man? And should it not be the aim of education to help us learn what that end, that desirable state of being, is, and how to attain to it as far as the imperfect nature of man will allow?

We have been "doing" for three hundred years. We have cleared and settled a continent. We have accumulated the most colossal store of material power and resources the world has ever seen. Is it not time that we began to think what to do with all our means, what the end is that we wish to attain? If we are not to do it *now*, when, in Heaven's

name, are we *ever* going to be rich and prosperous enough
to do it? We have always given as an excuse for our cultural
barrenness that we have had to lay the material foundations
first. But how can that excuse be given any more, when
we are the richest nation in the world, and we are told,
until we are almost sick of hearing it, that all classes enjoy
the highest standard of material comfort in the history of
the race? Are we forever to continue getting more things
in order to get more things with which to get more things,
and so on *ad infinitum*? Are we forever to seek the means
without ever considering the end for which we seek them?
Is there any sense in *doing* if we are never to *become* something, to *be* something, as a result? The entire practical life
in America urges us to do unceasingly and unthinkingly.
Should it not be one of the chief functions of education to
find the strands of meaning in our ceaseless web of doing
and to teach us some purpose in our lives? Can anything
give us that purpose better than culture, in the sense first
defined above? Can that culture be attained by a "liberal
education" that permits "business organization," "fire insurance," "business psychology," or "personnel administration"
to be substituted at the whim of the student for literature,
art, science, history or philosophy?

Does not our whole educational muddle spring in part
from mob snobbery—from exactly the same mental attitude
that makes the laboring class talk of "colored wash-ladies"
and "garbage gentlemen," that makes them want to be
dubbed Bachelors of Art after studying business English
and typewriting, ever gaining heaven by serving earth?
Does it not also spring in part from the lack of character
and of a coherent philosophy of life among those who should

be our educational leaders? To the latter, in taxes and endowments, we are giving money reckoned in hundreds of millions. We are giving them also a hundred million years or so of the lives of our young in every generation. In exchange, what are they returning to us in national ideals and culture? Is it not a fair question?

CHAPTER VIII
MASS PRODUCTION AND INTELLECTUAL PRODUCTION

MASS PRODUCTION AND INTELLECTUAL PRODUCTION

Education in America, where there are about seven hundred thousand students in institutions of collegiate rank alone, has become almost a major industry. Although teachers are not yet organized into trade unions there is a greater cohesion among them as a body than there is among artists, journalists, clergymen, authors, and other men leading what may loosely be called the artistic or intellectual life. Moreover it is easier to get at the economic situation of the professor's household than it is to do so in the case of the others. Statistics of income are readily available and, thanks to two recent studies, one made of the faculty of Yale and the other of that of the University of California, we have very definite information as to their detailed expenses. For these various reasons the question of the professional income of the intellectual worker and its relation to the general wage or income scale of the country and the standard of living has largely been confined to the teacher. For the same reasons the teacher offers perhaps the best starting point for a present discussion of our problem.

The California study[1] was a survey of the incomes, expenses, and ways of life of ninety-six married members of the faculty, and I shall attempt to summarize only a few of the salient points brought out by the investigation. Half

[1] Getting and Spending at the Professional Standard of Living. By J. B. Peixotto. New York: The Macmillan Co._ 1927.

of these families had one child or none and the entire ninety-six averaged one and a half children per family. As a rule the salaries did not cover the necessary living expenses, the median salary of the whole group amounting to only sixty-five per cent of its total income (mostly spent), the difference being made up almost wholly from extra earnings and not from investments. The salaries ranged from $1,400 to $8,000, the average being $3,000; the bulk of the men holding full professorial rank being paid from $4,000 to $5,000. In forty per cent of the families the wives worked and added to the family income. As a rule, the men found teaching in the summer the only way of making the additional amount called for by their expenses, so that one-third of the faculty members and their wives reported no vacation at all; forty per cent had less than two weeks; and sixty per cent less than four weeks.

Correlating salaries and length of service, we find that after four years at college and three to five years additional preparation working for a higher degree or as a teaching fellow, a man may serve on the faculty from twelve to twenty-five years and be close to fifty years of age before he is at all assured of getting from $3,000 to $4,000, even if he is retained and successful. After fifteen years' service on top of from seven to nine years' preparation, he has one chance in ten of earning from $5,000 to $7,000. Fourteen years' service, or twenty-one to twenty-three in all, are required to bring him to security of tenure on a salary of from $4,000 to $5,000. No family spending less than $6,000 was able to afford a full-time maid. Nearly one-third of the wives, mostly college-bred themselves, did all of the family laundry as well as the rest of the housework. For two-thirds of the husbands and one-half of the wives, clothing was reported as costing annually between $100 and $200 each. The average amount spent per family for recreation, other than an automobile, was $200 a year. As a result of the study the investigator reaches the conclusion that $7,000 is the minimum amount per year on which a professional family can live without impairing their own efficiency in their professional work.

The findings at Yale are equally striking. The official report[1] made on conditions there recites, with regard to the members of the faculty spending $4,000 a year, that "the married men at this level are usually of assistant professor rank, often with families of young children. They must live with extreme economy in the cheapest obtainable apartment, borrowing to meet the expenses of childbirth or sickness. The wife does all the cooking, housework, and laundry." Of those spending $8,500 the report states that "the families of associate professors and the younger full professors at this level, with three children and school expenses from nothing up to $1,000 a year, may either have a full-time servant or spend only $200 to $400 for occasional service. They live on the edge of a deficit. Even a small insurance premium is paid with difficulty and the purchase of clothing is kept as low as possible." More than a quarter of the faculty families covered by the report had no children, and the average number of children in such families as had any was exactly two. An instructor for the first two years

[1]Incomes and Living Costs of a University Faculty. Edited by Y. Henderson and M. D. Davis. New Haven: Yale University Press. 1928.

gets a salary of $1,500-$1,800, in his third year $2,100, and thereafter $2,500. An assistant professor gets $3,000 during his first three years, $3,500 in the next three years, and $4,000 during his next three. An associate professor gets from $4,000 to $5,000 and a professor from $5,000 to $8,000. A first-class cook in New Haven costs about $1,000 a year. Summing up, the report adds that "taking into account the expenses to which his position subjects him and judging by the home that he is able to maintain, the American university teacher in many cases lives essentially as do men of the skilled mechanic class. . . . It would perhaps be generally conceded that a reasonable standard for the economic level for a professor after twenty-five years of service would be the amount of money necessary to maintain a home in a ten-room house, which he owns free of mortgage, to keep one servant and pay for some occasional service, and to provide an education for his children in preparatory school, college, and professional school on an equality with that obtained by the general run of students in this University. From the costs of various modes of living shown above [in the report], it appears that life at this level in New Haven now comes to about $15,000 or $16,000 a year."

It is well known to those familiar with the situation of other intellectual workers that they find themselves in the same plight as the teachers in every case in which they do not sell their product in a mass-market, but before carrying the argument further I must touch on one more point in connection with the teachers. In another recent report[1] covering 302 colleges with 11,361 faculty members, it is

[1] Teachers' Salaries 1926-7. By Trevor Arnett. General Education Board. 1928.

stated that the average salary paid instructors, assistant or associate professors, and professors was $2,958. This compares with $1,724 in 1914–15. If we take that year as par and accept the usual comparison of the value of the dollar now as 61.7 cents, we find that in purchasing power the present average salary is $1,825, or about six per cent more than eleven years previously. It is evident therefore that the present crisis and deep discontent among intellectual workers is not due, or due only in small part, merely to the depreciated value of money. We must seek the cause elsewhere.

It is due in my opinion mainly to two things, both of which derive largely from mass production, namely, a rapidly altered standard and ideal of living, and a vast and equally rapid shift in the economic positions of the various classes of society.

Mass production, for the manufacturer, greatly decreases the cost of production, and selling in vast quantities greatly increases profits. There will come a time for almost every product when the inertia of selling it in a market already fairly saturated with it will increase the selling cost to such an extent as may more than equal the decreased cost of production, as is already occurring in certain lines. But meanwhile mass production has created enormous profits. In some cases and to some extent, though much fewer and less than generally assumed, the consumer has shared in these profits through lowered retail prices. The rest of the increased profit has gone in part to the workmen and, in much larger part, to the owners of the plants. In some lines, notably ready-made clothes for men, the prices of which are two and a half times those of 1912, the consumer has not benefited at all.

A generation ago the range of goods which even the rich might buy was comparatively restricted, and the scale of expenditure for practically every one was moderate. Today there is an almost unlimited range, and although mass production may have put innumerable things at the disposal of the public, the cost of living has not only been enormously increased by them (as in the case of the automobile which absorbed on the average six per cent of the total expense of the University of California faculty), but the constant assault on people's minds by the most insidious sort of advertising makes these things appear necessities. Mass production requires mass sales, and mass sales require that the public shall be made to believe in the necessity of buying. The ideal of the modern business man is not to supply wants but to create them. America has always been a mass-minded country, and the modern sales manager not only appeals to the individual in creating new wants but enlists on his side the whole force of social opinion. His effort is directed not only at making an individual desire a certain article for itself but at making him feel that his standing in the community and the welfare of his wife and children depend upon their having it.

Mass-production salesmanship thus develops throughout all society a vast number of new and formerly unfelt wants, wants based on the things themselves or on social prestige. If these wants are satisfied by purchase the family expense is greatly increased. If the individual resists when others of his own class, and more particularly those formerly considered as in a lower social or economic class, buy freely, he feels himself sinking in the social scale in a country in which the "standard of living" has come to have wholly a material significance. Moreover, many of these new things, such as the automobile and telephone, become literal necessities, when they become so common as to create a new social life based upon their possession. As I pointed out in an earlier chapter a very considerable part of the increased cost of living is due to the so-called higher scale of living, so that a comparison between the increase of salaries and the increase in the cost of certain goods is no indication at all of the increased difficulty of living.

The scientific inventions and new commercial products of the past twenty years would, in any case, have made their appeal to such classes in the community as could have afforded them, but the complete change in the American mode of life and the consequent cost which has engulfed us all like a tidal wave would not have occurred had it not been for mass production. No one is troubled by not having something of which he has never heard, and he is not greatly so by not being able to have something which no one has whom he is ever likely to know personally. For example, it could not have troubled a college professor or writer in 1890 that he had not an automobile. It does not trouble him today that he cannot have a private five-hundred-foot ocean-going yacht like Vincent Astor. It is not wholly a question of keeping up with the Joneses. Having a $2,000 car when one ought to have only a Ford is sheer ostentation, but having some car in the country is now a necessity unless one is going to cut one's self and one's family off from a very large part of social "neighborhood" as well as from the pleasures that all one's friends, practically without exception, are enjoying. The fact that today "everyone is having everything," whether they pay for it or not, is due to advertising and "high-powered salesmanship," and these are due primarily to mass production which requires mass markets.

But even these would not have been sufficient to alter so completely the status and peace of mind of the intellectual worker had it not been for the other effect of mass production mentioned above, that is, the shift in the economic status of the other classes. Formerly, although the intellectual worker occupied a comparatively low position in the economic scale, he was distinctly above the laboring class, and even between him and the successful business man there was no unbridgable gulf. Between the home of the college professor, clergyman, or author and that of the business man there was a difference in degree but not in kind. The intellectual, like his business acquaintance, could have decent living quarters for his family and a maid to relieve his wife of the heaviest household duties, and make his home an expression of himself.

Today the intellectual finds his life and status attacked both from above and below. Whatever may be the other and somewhat problematic results of mass production, it has assuredly made the rich incredibly richer than they ever were before. Ford, who has refused an offer of one billion dollars, cash for his plant, and who, in his incorporated form, keeps a balance at the bank of four hundred millions, is only a glaring example of what has been going on all around us. The same figures that represented the entire capital values of considerable fortunes twenty years ago represent today but the annual incomes of the fortunate transient war profiteers or permanent mass producers. This colossal increase in the wealth of the wealthy is tending to place a complete gulf between classes and at the same time to establish unprecedented standards of living.

Though it may seem a minor matter, take for example the question of furnishing a home. If the laws of imitation are of great power in society, so is that which makes expressing one's own personality one of the joys of life. The masters of mass production may preach the benefits of standardization but they themselves are exempt from the process. "A standardized print on your wall is just the thing for you," say they, while, like Mr. Mellon, they are reported to bid Count Czernin a million dollars for a Vermeer. "Standardized furniture is just the thing for the home," they preach from magazines while they sweep the market clean, at fabulous prices, of the fine old bits that even the most modest collector might have hoped to pick up with luck twenty years ago, until they have forced even the richest museums to forgo purchase. The intellectuals, because they are intellectual, are among the most insistent of human beings against being standardized. The mass production managers feed them Ford cars, Victrolas, cheap prints and other forms of *panes et circenses* and tell them they should be satisfied, while they themselves by the power of their wealth, and in their frantic endeavor to escape standardized homes for themselves, bid fantastic prices against one another for old silver, chairs, tables, pictures, and every product of non-machine-made art and artisanship. The average man today, who wishes to make his home, sees everything but standardized articles soaring into the financial heavens above like toy balloons escaped from a child's hand. It is symptomatic of much else in a new world suffering from colossal and concentrated wealth. The intellectual finds himself deprived of more and more in comparison with the business man, and shoved downward into the general undistinguished standardized mass.

But if he is shoved downward by the effect of the mass production wealth above him, he also has had a serious blow from the mass production wages of the classes below him. All wages have felt the effects of the mass production scales, and the result is that while the wealthy can pay the $900 or $1,000 demanded by a maid, the intellectual worker's wife does the cooking and laundry, as we saw above. Is it any wonder, as a man watches his wife, who perhaps has as good a mind as his own, spend her days over the range and the tub in order that he may use his own mind to the best advantage, that he wonders what is ahead for her and the children and meditates escape for all of them from the plight into which they have been plunged? In a less material civilization, such as that of France, where, moreover, intellectual work has social recognition and reward quite apart from its financial, the plight is in many respects less serious even in the face of what Americans would consider poverty.

Such an escape, as we have just suggested, however, if made, has two aspects, the individual and the social. Frequently it is not difficult to make. It may be a complete flight from the intellectual to the business world, as has been and is being made by many. Or it may take the form of adapting one's intellectual product to mass consumption. One may try for the movies, preach sensational sermons, become a popular lecturer, write text books, or, if one has been writing for the serious magazines, try to learn the trick of writing for those with circulation in millions; and quadruple one's income or even amass a fortune. All the methods of escape suggested, however, entail for the individual a warping of the characteristic bent of his mind and generally a serious degeneration in his intellectual quality and character.

The escape thus has its social aspect. America already has, probably, the lowest grade mental life of any of the great modern nations. It can ill afford to destroy what intellectual life it has and force all intellectual and artistic individualism into the mass pattern. At the end of that road lies an Assyria, a Babylon, a Carthage. Not only can a nation not continue to function humanely with a large part of its intellectual life suppressed, but it may be asked whether it can permanently continue to function at all. The rich may buy up all the old furniture and paintings in the world, but without new mind it would seem as though a machine civilization based on science must perish. All of our practical business men and inventors are now dependent in the last analysis on the pure scientist, the man whose thought and experiments bear no apparent relation to the practical life. The business man may consider the intellectual a crank and of no account in a practical world unless he submits to mass production and rolls up royalties that can be understood even by a realtor, but the intellectual life is all of a piece and it may be questioned whether a nation that gauges its values by purely material standards and yet at the same time reduces its intellectual workers below the economic level of a freight-car conductor can continue indefinitely to produce even the pure scientist. As M. Herriot said in an address to the students of the Sorbonne last July, "ne croyez pas à l'artificielle distinction des sciences et des lettres. . . . Les faits sont innombrables et les formes infinies. Au-dessus de tout, il y a l'esprit, maître du monde."

Europe might supply us with ideas in exchange for dollars but I see no remedy for our own intellectual life except a gradually growing sense of the real values of civilization on the part of the people. If business men consider a railway conductor a more important person than a professor, they will, quite apart from the law of supply and demand, give him a larger salary, and provide for college buildings rather than for the men who alone can give the buildings any significance. The problem comes back, as most do, to what people consider the real values in life. If, in the overwhelming mass of the population, those values are material and not spiritual, one cannot expect the spiritual life to flourish.

Of course for the intellectual worker of any sort, Grub Street has always been in the background, and a teacher, writer, or artist is probably further removed from the fear of starvation and the gutter today than perhaps ever before. It may also be conceded that the intellectuals should lead the way in renunciation and a sane ordering of life. But it must be remembered that in America owing to mass *mores* the individual (with his family) is infinitely less free to lead his own life in his own way and yet retain social contacts with others than he is in almost any country in Europe. To a considerable extent, it is only after he has conformed to the material American standards that his real spiritual freedom and influence in personal relationships, begin. Moreover, whereas in Europe one can both preach and practise renunciation of the material for the sake of the spiritual, the doctrine in this country is considered un-American, and if carried out by many would obviously bring the whole system of mass production crashing about our ears. This is readily understood by the business leaders, who are the real heroes and ideals of the people. The last thing in the world that they want either preached or practised is the simple life. The intellectual here, therefore, who is himself quite content to live that life and do his creative work without any thought of competing for rewards with the business man, finds solidly aligned against such a scheme of living not only the mass production wage scales which make the cost of almost any decent living prohibitive, but also the opinion of a spiritually unawakened public singularly bent upon forcing conformity to its own standards, and the opinion of the interested leaders of the public, the business men whose own profits now depend upon the public's becoming more and more materialistic.

The gigantic powers of manufacturing now in existence require for their profitable exploitation that the public shall be made steadily to develop new wants, wants that can be satisfied only by manufactured articles. Hoover and others may prate all they like about the concurrent need of an intellectual and spiritual life, but how is that life to develop if people are to be made to use their whole energies in satisfying new wants on the material plane? Yet if, on the one hand, they do not so grow, and, on the other, the intellectual classes become steadily more pinched between the two classes benefiting by mass production,—the owners above setting ever higher standards of living and the operatives below pressing steadily past them in an orgy of material well-being,—what will become of the intellectuals and how long will they continue to struggle and deny themselves, and have their wives do the laundry, in a civilization which will more and more look down upon their lack of earning power and their declining economic and social status?

CHAPTER IX
THE MUCKER POSE

THE MUCKER POSE

I

This borrowed title expresses better than any I have been able to devise for myself a problem which has recently been put to me by several of my American friends, men who on account of both their profession and positions are familiar with the more cultured portion of the American scene. The question which they put is one that I have been hesitatingly asking myself as I contrast that scene on successive returns from abroad with the one very obviously to be observed in this respect in France or England. "Why," they ask, "is it that a gentleman in America nowadays seems afraid to appear as such; that even university men try to appear uncultured; and that the pose of a gentleman and a scholar is that of the man in the street?" A few nights ago another friend of mine, a literary editor of some importance in New York, complained in the course of the evening's talk that the verbal criticism of many of the writers whom he knew had descended to the moronic classifications of "hot stuff," "bully," "rot," and so on. These writers, often meticulous in the artistry of their own work and thoroughly competent to criticize acutely and intelligently that of others, appeared afraid to do so lest they be considered as literary poseurs. The real pose in their cases was in talking like news-agents on a railroad train; but that appeared to them to be safe, whereas vague danger lurked in conversing as would any intelligent French or English critic.

The mucker-poseurs do not content themselves with talking like uneducated half-wits. They also emulate the language and manners of the bargee and the longshoreman, although where the profanity of the latter is apt to have at least the virtue of picturesqueness, the swearing of the mucker-poseur is apt to be merely coarse. A member of a most distinguished family and a young graduate of one of our best known Eastern universities was overheard the other day in his university club in New York describing his new position in the banking world. The nearest to analysis or description of his work that this young scion of American aristocracy with every social and educational advantage could reach was to tell his friends that it was "the Goddamnedest most interesting job in the world." Among both men and women of the supposedly cultivated classes such profanity is much on the increase. I know of a man who has recently declined to take foreign visitors to his club for luncheon or dinner any longer on account of the unfortunate impression which would be made upon them by the hard swearing of the American gentlemen, mucker-poseurs, at the surrounding tables. One of the finest scholars in the country, a man who once had distinguished manners, has become not only extremely profane but exceedingly addicted to smutty stories, both, apparently, in the effort to make himself considered a good mixer and as a bid for popularity. If one wishes to acquire an extensive and varied vocabulary of the most modern sort, one has merely to watch the young ladies of the mucker-poseur type playing tennis at Southampton or Newport.

Again, the mucker-poseur aims to act like the lowest of muckers when he—and frequently she—gets drunk. Drinking in this country has ceased to add any charm or grace to social life. On a sailing from New York on the *Aquitania* at midnight I counted twelve first-cabin women passengers brought on board, all so drunk that they could not get up the gangway without help. Many years ago, when I was a small boy of twelve, I attended "Field Day" at one of the most exclusive private boarding schools in the East. In the course of the day an address was made by an old graduate on the subject of alcohol. To the surprise and horror of the clerical head of the school, the good-natured but somewhat inebriated speaker said nothing to condemn drinking, but he threw out the comment, which is all I can now recall of his speech, that "when you boys do drink, remember always to get drunk like gentlemen." That is something which our present generation of drinkers have completely forgotten. They act in country clubs in a way which would have been considered a disgrace to the patrons and patronized in a disorderly house of a generation ago. It is a question not of a mere decline in manners but of consciously striven-for pose.

In the case of the young this is more understandable, just as it is more international. I am not here concerned, however, with (or at) the vagaries of the younger and, in so many respects, admirable generation. I am concerned with their elders, men who have lived long enough to have developed personalities of their own, men who appreciate the value of cultivating both mind and manners. Why should they be afraid to appear as cultured gentlemen and assume as a protective coloration the manners and level of thought of those who are beneath them?

The question would be a futile one unless we believed that manners and culture possess genuine significance, a significance for society as a whole as well as for the individual. It is all too evident that a large proportion of the dwellers in our United States do not believe so, but there is a large minority which does. Not to do so argues a failure to think things through and ignorance of history and human nature. This chapter deals with the contemporary attitude of many believers, and we can but glance briefly, before passing to them, at the non-believers.

II

One of the most suggestive methods of modern study has been the comparative. By the use of none other, however, are the unwary and the untrained so likely to come to logical grief over a *non sequitur*. The comparative study of habits and customs has revealed that both moral and social conventions have varied from age to age, from place to place, and from race to race. Immediately the unwary and untrained jump to the conclusion that because there appear to be no eternal or universal standards of morals and manners there is, therefore, no value in a local, temporary, and but slowly changing one—a conclusion by no logical possibility to be drawn from the premises. The result of this particular and, at the moment, very popular *non sequitur* has been to cause in many persons a headlong jettisoning of their whole cargo of morals, manners, and conventions, and the bringing about of a muckerly chaos which arouses mirth or terror according to the temperament of the social observer.

It would seem as though no sane person with a knowledge of the past of his own species and any adequate insight into human nature could fail to believe in the absolute need of *some* standards, *some* established values, to save us from a derelict wallowing about in the welter of sensations, impulses, attractions, and repulsions which form so much of this strange dream we call life. The standards, the values, will undoubtedly alter from time to time and from place to place; but that does not invalidate the need of having some of them at any one given time and place. Even the now much scorned minor conventions have their effective influence upon conduct, remote or proximate. A story is told of an English gentleman who was sent out as governor of an island where the entire population save for his sole self was black and savage. He dressed for his solitary dinner every night as carefully as though he were about to take a taxi to the smartest residence in Park Lane. He did so not from habit but from a knowledge of human nature. "If," he said, "I should drop this convention of civilized society, I should find myself some day having dropped one and another of the more important conventions, social and moral, and lower myself to the level of the blacks whom I govern. Evening clothes are far more important here than they ever were in London."

As for the second point, lack of culture, it is most evident in the extreme slovenliness in America in the use of the English language. There is, of course, some slang which is not slovenly but which has been born in a flash of genuine insight; and the language is always being enriched by absorbing many such words from below, much as the English aristocracy is by marrying or admitting commoners. But this is not true of the vast mass of slang words and cheap and easy expressions which are intellectually slovenly and nothing else; and anyone habitually using them impairs the keenness of his mind as much as he would the strength of his body by lolling in a hammock all his life. There is no question but that slang, hackneyed phrases, and clichés worn smooth make for intellectual laziness, and if constantly used blur the sense of discrimination. The very first step toward a cultivated mind is the development of the ability rationally to discriminate, to distinguish between varying values and qualities. It is not easy, and most of us Americans rarely achieve it in the cultural field. I have often been struck by the different replies one receives from an American and a Frenchman if you ask them what sort of person so-and-so is. The American will usually find himself helpless and toss off a mere "good scout," "a great guy," "a good egg," whereas the Frenchman, with a moment's reflection, will give you in half a dozen sentences a sharply etched sketch of the man's distinctive characteristics, or what he believes to be such, and classify him accurately as to type. To describe anything accurately— book, picture, man or woman—so as to bring out its unique individual qualities, calls for mental exercise of no mean order. One has to train one's self to do it and keep in training; yet the ability to distinguish, if one of the first steps toward culture, is also, in its higher forms, one of its most perfect fruits. If one dodges every call for discrimination, if one gets no farther in describing a book than "hot stuff," one loses the power after a while even if one ever possessed it. Slovenly language corrodes the mind.

These few observations as to manners and culture are well enough understood by any cultivated person who has had social and intellectual training and who has thought things through. He knows that there are both values and dangers in life, that some things are more valuable than others, and that if he has achieved any such social and intellectual training he cannot lower himself to the general level again without risk. If manners and culture have no value, there is no question involved, but if they have—and we shall now assume that they have—the man who possesses them is above, in those respects at least, the vast mass of men who do not possess them. Why then should he pretend not to, and assume the manners and mental lazzaronism of the crowd? It may be that there is no answer to the question, but as I find those better qualified than myself asking it, it is worth pondering over, and I have come to think that there may be three fundamental influences at work in America which will help us to solve it. One is democracy as we have it, another is business, and the third is the extreme mobility of American life.

III

In civilization no man can live wholly to or for himself, and whoever would achieve power, influence, or success must cater to the tastes and whims of those who have the granting of these things in their hands. In a democracy, speaking broadly, those who have the power to grant are the whole people; and the minds and manners of the people as a whole are of necessity below those of the chosen few who have risen above the average level by gifts of nature or happy opportunity. Every social class everywhere has always had its own standards of morals, manners, and culture. When such classes are separated by wide social or economic chasms, the only influences they exert upon one another are apt to be negative. Each lives in a world of its own, supported by the only public opinion for which it cares, that of its own class. Each also tends to react against the manners or morals of the other. The aristocrats of an earlier day looked down upon the common people and were more than ever satisfied with their own codes. The common people, in turn, feeling themselves despised, bolstered up their egos by despising the manners and morals of the class which looked down upon them. Much of the Puritan movement in England and elsewhere has here its roots. By no possibility could an ordinary laborer attain to the manners, social ease, or knowledge of the world of a duke. Ergo, the laborer, by unconscious mental processes well understood by modern psychology, asserted his own worth by denying worth to the qualities of the classes above him. He could not have the manners of a duke; therefore, those manners were undesirable anyway. He could not travel and he could not gain the most valuable sort of education, that of association with great or cultivated men; therefore, such things were of no importance. So long as the classes remain separated, as I said above, their influence upon one another is largely negative, but when class distinctions disappear in a democracy the mutual influences of members of those former classes or their vestiges in later generations become as complex in their action as the currents where tide and river meet.

The effects of democracy in America have been emphasized by three factors not present in any of the great democracies of Europe. In the first place, the Americans started almost wholly fresh. Here were no thousand-year-old institutions and forms of government and society to be reckoned with as impediments. America was a clean slate. The settlers did indeed bring with them habits, information, and memories gained in the Old World, but they brought them to a wilderness.

In the second place, America has been built up exclusively by the middle and lower classes, from which practically all of us have descended. Scarcely a man has ever come and settled here who did not belong to one or the other; and the most distinguished American families form no exceptions. Every class in history has had its good and bad attributes which have varied with class, country, and period. The English middle class, upper and lower, from which the character of America, with some modifications, has essentially been built up, had admirable qualities, but it lacked some of those enjoyed by the aristocracy. For our purpose here we need mention only one. The genuine aristocrat insists upon being himself and is disdainful of public opinion. The middle class, on the other hand, has always been notoriously timid socially. It rests in terror not only of public but even of village opinion. If the religious refugees of New England be held an exception, it may be noted that the genuine ones were far fewer than used to be supposed, and that as a whole the New England immigration may be considered as part of the great economic exodus from England which took thirty thousand Englishmen to Barbados and little St. Kitts while only twelve thousand were settling Massachusetts. Religious refugees have formed an infinitesimal part of American immigration as compared with the economic ones.

The third great influence upon American democracy has been the frontier, whose line was lapped by the waves of the Atlantic in 1640 and after retreating three thousand miles to the Pacific was declared officially closed only in 1890. In the hard, rough life of the frontier manners and culture find no home. As Pastorius, the most learned man who came to America before 1700, said, "never have metaphysics or Aristotelian logic earned a loaf of bread." When one is busy killing Indians, clearing the forest, and trekking farther westward every decade, a strong arm, an axe, and a rifle are worth more than all the culture of all the ages. Not only has the frontiersman no leisure or opportunity to acquire manners and culture but, because of their apparent uselessness, and in true class spirit, he comes to despise them. They are effete, effeminate, whereas he and his fellows are the "real men." The well-dressed, cultivated gentleman becomes the "dude," object of derision, who, so far from exerting any ameliorating social or intellectual influence, is heartily looked down upon; and culture itself is relegated to idle women as something with which no real man would concern himself.

These are some of the special attributes of American democracy, and of any democracy in a new land, which it shows in addition to those it would show in any case merely as a democracy. In America it was slow in gathering into its hands the reins of power. For many generations the

English aristocratic tradition in part survived, and it may be recalled that we were a part of the British Empire for a longer period than we have been independent. In general, the "appeal to the people" throughout the colonial period and the years of the early republic was an appeal to "the best people" only. The first two presidents, Washington and Adams, were as little democratic in doctrine as they were by nature. Jefferson's doctrinal democracy was largely offset in practice by his being an aristocrat to his finger tips by nature, and it was not until Andrew Jackson that "the people" in the democratic sense came into their own. At his inaugural reception in the White House his followers climbed upon the silken chairs in their muddy boots to get a look at him, rushed the waiters to grab champagne, broke the glasses, and in the joy of victory gave a number of ladies bloody noses, and even the President himself had to be rescued from his admirers and hurried out through a back door. This historic episode may be taken to mark the turning-point in American manners. These people had made a President. Thereafter their tastes would form one of the national influences.

IV

It is this new democracy, a hundred times richer and a shade less raw, which is in the saddle to-day. What has it done in the way of influencing manners and thought? Leaving all else aside, even at the risk of drawing a false picture, we shall consider only those points which may help to answer our first question. For one thing, then, it has knocked the dignity of its elected officials into a cocked hat. Leav-

ing out of the scene many of its chosen, such as the mayor
of Chicago or its favorite, Bryan, it forces a man to play the
mountebank and, whatever the character of the man himself, to appear as one of "the people." Washington was a
very human man but he never forgot that he was a gentleman. He was adored by his soldiers, but he won their deep
affection without ever for a moment losing the dignity of
his character and manner. One has only to imagine what
would have happened had a group of his men shouted
"Atta Boy, Georgie!" to realize the gulf between his day
and ours. When John Quincy Adams was President, he
declined to attend a county fair in Maryland, remarking
privately that he did not intend that the President of the
United States should be made a sideshow at a cattle fair.
To-day, the people insist that the President be a side-show;
and Roosevelt, with amused understanding, in his cowboy
suit and his Rough rider uniform, used his "properties"
as does an actor. Even the supremely conventional Coolidge
had to dress up in a ten-gallon hat and chaps, although
utterly out of character, and looking so. Just as I write
these lines, my attention is called to an announcement in
large type in this morning's *New York Times* that it will
publish next Sunday "photographs of Herbert Hoover in
workaday clothes and a panorama of his ranch." So he, too,
is cast for the comedy. Democracy cracks the whip, and
even the most conservative of candidates and officials must
dance. In the campaign of 1916 it is said that Hughes was
politely asked to shave his beard to suit the people. He
balked and consented only so far as to trim it. But then
he lost the election.

The people want officials in their own image. Such men as Elihu Root, Joseph Choate, or John Hay are rarely elected, only appointed. To get anywhere in elective politics one must be a "good mixer," and to be a good mixer one must shed a good part of one's culture and a good part of one's manners. Dignity to a considerable degree must be discarded. One must conceal one's knowledge of English and learn the vernacular, except for "orations." Henry Adams, when he became a newspaper correspondent in Washington, said that he had to "learn to talk to Western congressmen and to hide his own antecedents." It is what every gentleman who desires to take part in elective public life on a large or small stage in the country to-day has to do to some extent except for happy accidents.

Our democracy has fostered education, at least to the extent of almost fabulously increasing the numbers of the reading public. What has been, for the purpose of the present argument, the effect of that? There has been one effect, at least, germane to this discussion. It has greatly lowered the tone of our public press. Such newspaper men as I know agree with me that there has been a most marked decline even in the last twenty years, and they agree with me as to the cause. In the old days a newspaper was largely a personal organ, and what appeared in it reflected for good or ill upon the editor, who was known by name to all its readers. In New York the *Sun* was Charles A. Dana. The *Tribune* was Horace Greeley. To-day we know no editors, only owners. The newspaper of to-day aims only at circulation, and with every increase in circulation the quality has to be lowered. The case is well known

of the purchaser a few years ago of what had been one of
the country's most distinguished journals, who told his
staff that thereafter they would have to "cut the highbrow"
and write down to the level of the increased public he intended to go after. First the "yellow press," then the
tabloids, taught the older newspapers what fortunes awaited
those who would stoop to pick them up by catering to the
masses. A newspaper depends on its advertising for its
profits. Advertising quantity and rates depend on circulation. Increased circulation spells decreased quality. There
is the vicious circle which has been drawn for us by the
huge mob which has become literate but not educated.

The discovery of the possibilities of mass circulation has
caused the advertisers to raise their demands. Some will
not advertise at all in journals with a circulation of less than
half a million. Advertising is withdrawn from those journals which heroically venture to maintain their quality at
the expense of not increasing their circulation. Financial
ruin usually results. The people are evidently getting the
kind of papers they want, but in doing so they are depriving
the cultured class of the sort *they* want, and used to get before America became so "educated." We get foreign cables
about the Prince of Wales dancing with Judy O'Grady, or
the doings of sex perverts in Berlin, and the treatment of
our domestic news is beneath contempt. The other night
I examined what used to be one of the leading papers not only
in New York but in the whole country and I found no head-
line on three consecutive pages which did not refer to scandal
or to crime. It has been said that the new reading public
has not interfered with the old, that there are simply vast
numbers of new readers of a different type who are being

supplied with what they want. That is not wholly true, and the competition of the new market has had a heavily detrimental influence on the older journals. To-day if a man wishes to succeed in a journalistic career on the daily press he has to scrap even more of his qualities as a gentleman and a scholar than he has to in a career of politics.

The democratic spread of education has also had detrimental effects in other ways. The necessity of finding instruction for the enormous numbers who now go to school, high school, and college has caused a demand for teachers which has far outrun the supply of those qualified to teach. Great numbers of these teachers have even less social and cultural background than have their students. Under them the students may learn the facts of some given subject, but they gain nothing in breadth of culture or even in manners. It is an old story that Charles Eliot Norton once began a lecture at Harvard by saying, "I suppose that none of you young men has ever seen a gentleman." The remark was hyperbolic, as was intended, but it is only too likely to-day that many young men can go through some of our newer "institutions of learning" without seeing at least what used to be called a gentleman. In the professions, more particularly medicine and law, complaint is rampant that they are being swamped by young men who know only the facts of the profession (when they know those) and have no cultural, ethical, or professional standards. A few such could be ignored. When they come, as they are coming now, in shoals, they lower the tone of the whole profession and, without standards themselves, force an unfair competition upon those who try to maintain them.

V

Perhaps the greatest pressure on the individual to force him to be wary of how he appears to others is in business, for the overwhelming mass of Americans are in the varied ranks of business of some sort or another. One who has reached the top and "made his pile" may, perhaps, do more or less as he pleases, subject only to milder forms of social pressure; but for those on the way the road is beset with pitfalls. Nearly every man wants to make himself popular with his employers, his fellow-workers, his office superiors, or his customers. These are made up of all sorts of men, but the sprinkling of gentlemen and scholars among them is so slight as to be almost negligible for the purpose of helping one's advancement. In America, to an extent known nowhere else, organization is used for every purpose. It is hardly too much to say that there can hardly be an American who is not a member of from one to a dozen organizations, ranging from Rotary, Lions, Kiwanis, Red Men, Masons, Mechanics, the Grange, and dozens more, to Bar Associations, Bankers' Clubs, and social and country clubs innumerable. Some of the larger corporations, notably the banks and trust companies in New York, now have clubs made up entirely of members of their own staffs, with obvious intent. In many lines of business the effect produced by one's personality at the annual "convention" is of prime importance. For business reasons it is essential that men should be at least moderately popular at all such organizations or meetings. On an unprecedented scale, tacitly understood but not openly acknowledged, there is competition for personal popularity. In many lines, such as stock brokerage where the service is almost wholly personal, it is needful to "play with your customers," the necessity varying not with their social congeniality but with the size of their account. In salesmanship of all sorts the results of the "personal approach" are, of course, of the first importance.

In order to gain popularity with a very large proportion of business men, many of whom have to-day risen from nothing to riches since the War, one thing is fundamentally necessary. You must never appear to be superior even if you are. Not long ago one of the New York banks added a new vice-president. He was chosen not for his ability but for his hearty vulgarity, so that he could "make contacts" with the bank's new sort of customers! Too perfect an accent in English may be almost as dangerous in business as a false one in Latin used to be in the House of Lords. To display a knowledge or taste in art or literature not possessed by your "prospect" may be fatal. On the whole, it is safest to plump yourself down to his level at once whatever that may be, to talk his talk, and only about what he talks. This pressure of the majority on one's personal tastes was amusingly exemplified to me one day when I was looking for a house to rent in a pleasant Jersey suburb. In the house shown me—as is the case in all the suburbs of New York I know—there was nothing to mark where my lawn might end and my neighbor's begin. All was as open to the public gaze as the street itself. I thought of delightful English or French gardens, surrounded by hedge or wall, screened from the public, where one could putter absurdly over one's plants, read one's book, or have one's supper as much to one's self as in the house. In fact they are out-door rooms, infinitely more attractive than the American "sun parlor." I knew well that no such attempt could be made here, but, nevertheless, I remarked to the "realtor" that it would be pleasant to have a hedge and privacy but I supposed it could not be done on account of the neighbors. "I say No," he answered with pained surprise, "if you are going to be 'high hat' you won't last long here." Just so, and so many things in this country are "high hat" which in other lands simply make for sane and cultivated living that it is no wonder that the business man whose car and cellarette, if not bread and butter, depend so often on his popularity, has to walk warily.

Just why having a garden-wall, speaking one's native tongue correctly, or being able to discriminate in matters of art or literature should be the Gallic equivalent of "high hat" would puzzle a Frenchman, but so it often is in the land of the free. And no one knows his way about the land of the free better than the business man. The pressure may vary with his position and the kind of business he is in, but in general he will soon discover that in any business where personal contact is a factor, the people with whom he deals and upon whose good will he has to lean will insist upon his not being too different from themselves. In Greenwich Village a man may wear a flowing tie and a Spanish hat, but it would be suicidal for a bond broker. One has to conform or one is lost. Our two most successful business men are perhaps John D. Rockefeller and Henry Ford. Rockefeller says it is a "religious duty" to make as much money as you can, and Ford has informed us that "history is bunk." The one standard of success in business—and perhaps its stark and easily grasped simplicity is what attracts many Americans—is the amount of money you make

from it. There are no foolish nuances. Most Americans
are business men. Whatever ideals they may have had in
college, and to a considerable extent whatever manners they
may have inherited or acquired, they begin to shed, unless
their niche is an unusually sheltered one, when the real
nature of the excoriating modern business competition dawns
upon them. Little by little as they "learn the game" they
conform to their customers or associates.

VI

Another characteristic of American life is its extreme
mobility. People move up and down in the social scale
and round about the country like bubbles in a boiling kettle.
Social life everywhere here is in a constant flux. I left Wall
Street, where I was in business, and a certain suburb where
I then lived, fifteen years ago. To-day the personnel of
"the Street" as I remember it is almost as completely
changed as are the symbols on the ticker. In the suburb
where I once knew everyone, at least by name, I know
scarcely half a dozen households. People are forever making
or losing money, arriving in new social sets, living in Pittsburgh or a mining camp one year and in Los Angeles or
St. Paul the next. This has a marked effect on social independence. When a family has lived for many generations
in the same place, or, as have many county families in England, for centuries, they acquire a social position almost
wholly independent of their individual members at a given
time. Indeed, a member is almost an accident and may be
as erratic and independent as he pleases. He still remains
a so-and-so of so-and-so, known to all the countryside. An

old hereditary title accomplishes the same result. Here and there in New England villages or in the South there are families who approximate this happy condition, but in the constant movement of the life of most Americans it is necessary for them to depend wholly upon the effect of their personalities and bank accounts. A man whose family has lived in the "big house" in a small Massachusetts town for a century or two is sufficiently "somebody" there almost to be independent; but should business require him to move to Kalamazoo he is nobody until he "shows them." The social reputation, immunity, and freedom which long residence in one place gives without effort or thought has to be built again from the ground up, and warily, when one moves to another town where they know not Joseph. One joins the organizations in the new town, and, again, one conforms. To begin in a new place by being "different" is dangerous; to begin by being too superior, even if actually, unconsciously, and with no wish to appear so, may be fatal. Like myself, had I gone to that Jersey suburb and made a little privacy round my garden, the newcomer might be voted "high hat" and not "last long."

In assuming the "mucker pose" the gentleman and scholar does not, of course, descend as low as the "mucker"; but he does, in self-defense, for the sake of peace and quiet, for business success, and for the sake of not offending the motley crowd of all sorts whom his neighbors are apt to be in the seething, changing society everywhere today, shed enough of his own personality not to offend the average. He avoids whatever others may think "high hat" in manners or culture as he would the plague. Like Henry Adams he will find

[214]

himself hiding his antecedents if they happen to be better than the neighbors'.

This possible answer to my friends' question does not necessarily indict democracy and American life. Both have brought new values into the world of other sorts. I am merely pointing to one of the possible losses. For it *is* a loss when a man deliberately uses worse manners than he knows how to use, when he tries to cover up his intellectual abilities, or when he tries to be average when he is above it. A business-democracy has accomplished a great task in levelling up the material condition of its people. It may be asked, however, whether there is no danger of a levelling down of manners and culture. Perhaps the new values gained offset the old ones in some danger of being lost, but it may, even in America, be left to one to question, to ponder, and to doubt. Is the mucker pose really forced on one? People adopt it, evidently, because they think it is the thing to do and essential to make them quickly popular. It does not always work, even in business. A dignified man of science was recently explaining to an applicant for a position some new research work he had been doing. The young Ph.D. was intensely interested. When the scientist concluded, he asked the flower of our highest university training what he thought of it. "Hot Dog!" was the immediate and enthusiastic answer, which, in this case, promptly blasted the young man's career in *that* laboratory. It would not have done so generally, however, and we come back to business as conducted to-day, and the character and background of our business leaders as, perhaps, the main contributing cause of forcing the mucker pose.

We can prate as we like about the idealism of America, but it is only money success which really counts. What are ideals or culture or charming manners as compared with business? What in the last presidential campaign did two leaders of opinion tell us, one from the Pacific and the other from the Atlantic coast? Mr. Hoover, in his address replying to the welcome given him by the people of San Francisco, told them that the most precious possession of their great city was—what?—*their foreign trade!* In New York, the *Sun* in its editorial explaining its intention to support the Republican party, admitted that the Prohibition question was "a live campaign topic," and that present conditions might be "intolerable" and "a morass of lawbreaking," but asked whether it was well to risk loss of prosperity for the possible reform of those conditions. In America to-day business life is not the basis for a rational social life, but social life is manipulated as the basis for an irrational business one. One makes acquaintances and tries for popularity in order to get ahead downtown. To an unprecedented extent the people who have money in all lines of business are newcomers from far down in the social scale, men with no culture and no background, and often no manners. We may note our new class of multi-millionaire landlords who have built fortunes out of shoe-strings since the War. Two of our now greatest industries have been wholly evolved in the last two decades, and one certainly does not look for culture among the kings in the motor and moving-picture trades. The "people" who came into political power under Jackson made a huge grab at economic power under Grant, but it has been reserved for the present to "make the world safe for democracy." The old class which had inherited manners

[216]

and culture as essential to an ordered life has abdicated mainly · for mere lack of funds. In business for the last decade it has been for the most part the conservatives, who had much to lose, who have lost, and the reckless who have won.

Business may explain the mucker pose, but it may be asked whether those who adopt it are not traitors to all that is best in the world and which has been so hardly built up. An impoverished aristocrat may sell his title in marriage for one generation to rehabilitate his house, but Americans who sell their culture and their breeding to truckle to the unbred in business, who shed these things of the spirit for motor cars and all the rest of the things of the body, are taking refuge in a yet more ignominious surrender. They may thus pick up some of the golden drippings from the muckers' tables, but they do not gain the respect of the muckers whom they imitate, and may yet awake to the fact that they have properly forfeited even their own.

CHAPTER X
MAY I ASK ?

MAY I ASK?

Our critics have often assured us that the dollar sign is the symbol of America. I am coming to the conclusion that our more characteristic one is the question mark. I have just typed them side by side on my Corona and have been looking at them. $ and ?. We may read the dollar sign as two parallel lines with a swirl trying to bring them together. One of these lines, as I see it, is expense and the other income. Parallel lines never meet in a Euclidean world. The S imposed on them represents the frantic effort of the individual to refute this geometrical finance. In this respect my present wanderings over a post-war world show me that there is nothing typically American about this symbol. The striving, the manifold tragedy, the wrung soul of an era concealed in this new swastika is universal. In England, France, Italy, Austria, Czecho-Slovakia, Holland, Belgium, —I find it wherever I have lately been, even when the expense line does not, as at home, insist upon describing a hopeless tangential curve away from its parallel. Once, however, one has finally escaped from the smoking room of the liner, landed at Southampton or Havre, Hamburg or Genoa and lost one's self among the "foreigners," one does escape from the question mark in its typical American repetitive usage.

One does not, it is true, escape entirely. The mails still function, and a good part of this long sunny afternoon which should have been devoted to work on my book, a stroll in the sunshine, or letters to old friends has been spent in my study typing answers to letters from strangers asking questions which any local librarian or even a little intelligent thought and work on the part of the questioners should have been able to answer for them. "Where can I find such-and-such a quotation?" "Ought I to encourage my son to become a teacher?" "What would be a good list of books to read?" "How can I make my boy take an interest in history?" As I respond as courteously as I can to this constant questioning from my native land, a usual part of my week's chores, I wonder what sort of minds ask all these and innumerable other questions. (One thing I know, and that is, I shall never be thanked, for it is a sad statistical fact that in ten years of answering questions from American strangers I have never but twice had even the courtesy of an acknowledgement of my reply. But that is beside the present point.)

That I am not alone in my pondering over this American question mark is indicated by another letter, lately received, from a man with a very different type of mind from the correspondents just noted. "A six weeks' lecture tour," he writes, "including Texas, California, and Colorado, brings me back to New York with the major impression that all America is asking questions. Healthy mental curiosity is not a thing to be condemned in children, but it is a healthier sign in adults when they occasionally take the trouble to think out the answers for themselves. My limited experience in France has convinced me that the average Frenchman is ashamed to ask a question without volunteering at least part of the answer. In England questions are apt to be either rhetorical or veiled in the form of statements open to correction. I am told the problem is the decay of conversation in America but I doubt whether we ever had any conversations to decay. Sophisticated New York is no exception."

Questions and converse are closely linked but it is easier in our social history to trace the continuance of the former than of the latter. We have, indeed, an occasional comment, such as that of John Adams who noted in his Diary when passing through New York in 1774 on his way to the Continental Congress that in spite "of all the opulence and splendor of this city, there is very little good breeding to be found" and "no conversation that is agreeable; there is no modesty, no attention to one another. They talk very loud, very fast, and all together." Alexander Hamilton, not the celebrated statesman but a Baltimore doctor, is the only man I know who tried to report colonial conversations verbatim, as may be found in his little-known but immensely entertaining *Itinerarium*. With almost complete unanimity, however, all travelers for a couple of centuries comment on the, to them, curious American habit of asking questions in every part of the country. It begins as early as 1710, perhaps earlier, and becomes marked as the travel literature rapidly increases after the French and Indian War. It is a habit, therefore, which obviously has a long history behind it and for which the first explanation sought must be an historical one.

The frontier, that omnipresent though often unrecognized influence in so many departments of American life, is probably at the bottom of it. In a sparsely settled section there are two good reasons for putting a stranger through his catechism,—danger and paucity of intellectual interest. Even today, in the remoter parts of the Carolina mountains, to quote a bit of personal experience, the opening of conversation is still stereotyped when a mountaineer meets a stranger on the road. "Howdy." Then, with no show of diffidence, "what mought your name be?", and when this has been satisfactorily answered, comes inevitably next, "whar mought you be goin'?".

Thus far the opening of the conversational game is evidently a cautious play for safety, so well understood that it is assumed no offence could possibly be taken. What, however, so many of the early American tourists complained of in New England and elsewhere, was the merciless catechising that followed,—questions as to one's age, married state, one's relatives, every imaginable detail of a personal sort by which the stranger's mind, history, circumstances and opinions were ruthlessly explored so long as he continued to submit. The American jaw possesses an idiosyncratic restlessness, which has been the foundation and prime cause of the rise of the Beeman, Adams, Wrigley and other gum fortunes, but I am inclined to trace the source of the second type of American questioning less to the extreme irritability of the maxillary muscles than to a psychological vacuity. The trick of questioning, instead of conversing, which developed among the dwellers in the towns, villages and frontier fringes of colonial America and which so disturbed the horde of French tourists who came to look us over following the Seven Years' and Revolutionary Wars, and the English who came from 1820 to 1850, was merely the rude effort of a primitive, predatory and half-starved brain to grab at food. The spider simply sucked the blood out of any insect that got caught in his web.

The community mental life of any village or provincial

town for most folk in the seventeenth and eighteenth centuries was hardly stimulating but, as compared with those
in Europe, that of the American towns, villages and lonely
clearings became a good deal like what the landscape must
have looked like after the last great thaw of the Ice Age
revealed it under the melted glacier. As I have pointed
out elsewhere, a struggle for life under primitive, even
savage conditions does not preclude the growth of an artistic
and intellectual life, as the arts and mythologies of any
primitive people from the African negroes to the Pacific
Islanders testify. What saps the white man and empties
his mind of all cultural elements when he struggles to subdue
a wilderness is the effort to maintain a civilized standard,
as far as possible, of material comfort under wilderness
opposition. Something has to be jettisoned from his cargo
or he sinks. He always naturally elects to throw culture
overboard until such time as, the storm weathered, he
thinks he may salvage it again. Hard as the life has been
in the old lands from which our first immigrants came,
English in New England, German in Pennsylvania, there had
been many means of self-expression and leisure, and a social
consciousness that made such self-expression natural. For example, among other things they brought with them their
arts and crafts. They carved the end beams of their houses,
painted designs on the overhang, designed, carved and
painted their furniture. Little by little all this was dropped.
The struggle proved too hard. A negro who lived in a grass
hut in the jungle had time to carve wooden sculpture, play
music, weave legends, but the white man who wanted in a
few years to make a European homestead out of a patch
of the American primeval forest had no leisure or surplus

energy for anything else. On the other hand, the struggle against new conditions sharpened his wits just at the time that he was throwing overboard everything that they could work on. They began to be ingrowing. In these new communities there was practically no diversification of labor or interest. Everyone was doing everything for himself, and almost all were doing just the same thing. On the voyages across from the old countries in the eighteenth century, the food supply frequently ran out and in some cases the immigrants actually ate each other. In the new communities to which they came, the mental food supply also ran out. There was often no food for conversation. It is not strange that they ate the strangers, mentally.

We thus have developed a working hypothesis as to where the question mark originated in American life. We will now consider its persistence. Why *does* it persist, and why, in the rich and diversified America of today, does not conversation takes its place?

For one thing, there is the inheritance from the past. The man who lived in a clearing or even a small village with no public library, newspapers, magazines or scarcely neighbors in the eighteenth century had some excuse for not giving his mind good food, and letting it get so starved that it would chew on anything that came its way. There can be literally scarcely an American today who has any such excuse for mental under-nourishment; but habits were formed. The American mind is full of the quaintest and most curious anomalies. In business, for example, it is the most radical and innovating mind (within the limits of the capitalistic system) in existence. Politically it is eighteenth century if not earlier. In the same way, the average American youth of either sex, though self-reliant socially to a marked and even startling degree, intellectually lacks, almost as markedly, all initiative. He, or she, studies his lessons and recites them, even in college, like good little grade boys and girls. The habit of wide-ranging intellectual curiosity and of self-reliance in satisfying it has been lost. The habit of asking questions has persisted. Everyone wants to be told what to read (mark the success of the book-clubs), what he should think, what is good and what is bad. Perhaps the most encouraging part of the Prohibition muddle is that it shows that at least he will kick and balk when told what he must drink. The first factor, then, is that the American mind has behind it no long habit of indulgence in intellectual curiosity, understood in the best sense. Through a long period it got out of the way of being interested in things other than those of the daily environment of work and play, or of the rag-tag and bob-tail of disconnected facts that might turn up with any stranger. There could be no more coherency among these than among the stray items one picks up by glancing through a popular magazine and a village newspaper. They kept the mind from eating into its own fibres, perhaps, but did nothing to train it as an instrument of thought.

Moreover, to a great extent, America is still provincial and frontier. I am not speaking solely of the international aspect of this. For the most part, it is, of course, utterly ignorant of the rest of the world. I am speaking generally and not of select groups. It is one of the quaint anomalies of which I spoke above, that the nation whose public mind is the least international of any of the great nations, should publish the best journal dealing solely with international affairs. That, however, has nothing to do with the case. The magazine is not self-supporting and has a limited circulation. The editor of several magazines of extremely wide circulation told me that they could publish nothing that did not directly deal with America, that their readers were interested in nothing else. The editor of another magazine, one of the best in the country, told me that, although for his own intellectual satisfaction he did occasionally publish an article on a foreign country, there was no reaction to it among his readers and as far as circulation went the pages might as well have been left blank.

It is not, however, in this sense only that I mean we are still provincial and frontier. In this sense, America is still in the frontier stage and it is becoming questionable if it will ever be anything else. The difference between the Indian and the Englishman was that the Englishman wanted all the physical comforts of old England set up in the wilderness in his own generation as fast as they could be. He measured his own minimum standard of living by that to which he had been accustomed or which he had seen. The attainment of this absorbing all his energy, he let the rest go. Could the first settlers of Boston in 1630 have seen the comfortable town of 1800, they would have believed that a settled, orderly and comely cultural life must surely by then have been attained. The trouble is that America never has attained. This, I well know, is by many considered as a virtue and I am discussing it here only from the standpoint of the main topic of this chapter.

The seaboard was soon comfortably settled, but the frontier kept extending and extending and absorbing the interest and energies of the people. In 1890 even the physical frontier was officially declared closed and ended by the government, but it made no difference, for the people were as busy and worn out as ever settling themselves in a wholly new country, the country of "the high standard of living." The settlers who two centuries ago had to jettison their cultural heritage and interests in order to cut down trees and snipe at Indians skulking behind those that had not yet been cut, have been replaced by the settlers in the Country of the High Standard who have to jettison their cultural tastes (the heritage has gone) in order to pay rent, get a cook, have two or three bathrooms and a motor car or two in this new frontier country of the Standard. They are just as pressed, hard-working and weary as their forefathers, and from the same reason,—trying to attain a standard of physical well-being to which they think they ought to attain in their own generation in an environment in which the old physical difficulties have merely been replaced by economic ones.

I have not, as yet, had a chance to read Mr. and Mrs. Lynd's *Middletown*, but it is, I understand, a very careful and not exaggerated study of a town of forty thousand people in the Middle West, yet a review says that it shows that "literature and art have virtually disappeared as male interests." It is what always happens in any frontier life, and America has replaced the old geographical frontier by the Living-standard one. In the old days, we used to tell critical foreigners that we had been so busy settling and subduing a continent that we had had no time for culture. Well, we have jolly well settled and subdued it. We have roped it, and thrown it, and eaten a good part of it up. But before we had time to get our breath we have gone off on a gold rush to this new land of the High Standard. Because it is on no map, there is no telling how big it is or how long it will take to settle and subdue it. Meanwhile the total energies of a good many of us are absorbed in "sawing wood" like our ancestors and protecting ourselves from the savages under the changed conditions imposed by settling this new country that can be found in no atlas. When the old frontier ended at the Pacific Ocean we had at least some limit set to the physical and mental energy necessary to make it habitable for civilized men, but one wonders to-day, as one swings one's economic axe and turns one's back on the shelf of books one would like to have time to read, where in heck is the Pacific Coast of this new country we have started to subdue.

This new country is a rushing, busy, hustling restless one. Not long ago I dined in America with an old friend I had not seen in some years. After dinner we walked into the library to have our coffee before the open fire. After we had sipped it and had a puff or two of our cigars, my host said, with the inevitability of after dinner New Yorkers, "Where do you want to go now?" I suggested that as I had not seen him for a long time I would much prefer to sit just where I was before the fire and talk to him. His reply was, "Thank Heaven. I haven't had a good talk with anybody in ages." Last year when home, a New York boy of about seventeen, a thoughtful lad, complained of his inability to find any men to talk with. "They always want to go somewhere or turn on the radio," he commented. "How is a boy to learn if he can never talk to a man?" At least for ordinary conversation, there used to be the home, the piazza in the evenings or the tramp through the country.

The motor car, the small apartment and the rest of the factors in the new high standard have largely done away with such opportunities. But I think that, as far as good conversation, and not mere talk, is concerned, these are surface symptoms, secondary influences.

Many elements are necessary for good conversation. For one thing there must be a sense of leisure. The talk may last only an hour, but an absence of any sense of hurry is essential. We may get through a business interview in five minutes, like rushing a bucket to a fire, but good talk should be like a stream on which we can float leisurely without knowing what may appear beyond the next bend. In order that there should be bends, however, each mind must have many interests. It is by no means necessary that the major interest of each of the talkers should be the same or even similar. As a rule, indeed, for the best of talk, it is just as well that they should not be. If they are, the talk is too apt to become and stay mere "shop." The talkers, however, must have backgrounds that afford ample points of contact. One must be able to range over fields of fact and thought without having forever to be adding interpretative footnotes.

It is the lack of this background that accounts in good part for the lack of conversation in America in the European sense, even among the professional and university classes. Too often in America as long as one keeps to a man's "subject" one may get a good deal that is interesting, even if it is imparted too much like a lecture, but once get off that and one is lost. It is like getting off a road in the dark. In contrast, I well recall an evening spent with a Frenchman, whose "subject" happens to be American history. As we had both written books known to the other on the topic,

[231]

we started on that, and I very soon found that he was better founded in it than many American professors. There was not a source to which I referred with which he was not well acquainted and which he did not quickly and accurately appraise. Soon the talk wandered to other matters. In a very amateurish way I had been interested in the Minoan civilization of Crete and had been to the Ashmolean Museum to hunt up some pottery. In a casual way he took up the question and discussed the various stages of the civilization and the changes in pottery design; and as we drifted from that to Greece and philosophy and literature, the talk flowed on and on, without effort or pedantry until we found it was one in the morning. He was, of course, a far abler and better educated man than myself, but outside of American history, perhaps, we were both amateurs in all we discussed. What I enjoyed was the breadth of the discussion, the wealth of background he had, the ability to illustrate some point by another in a wholly different field. It is just this that is lacking for the most part in American talk, which is apt to be narrow, professional, and all too often pedantic.

The European mind at its best is both fuller and more flexible than ours, though in many practical ways the American is perhaps the more flexible. It is not simply the number of facts absorbed but the play of mind and the fields covered. We have had our own examples of the scholar in politics, for example—the man of fairly wide interests, such as Wilson, Lodge, Roosevelt, to name three very different types; but they have been, so to speak, practical minds, working in history, law or natural science. We note the intrinsic difference when we run over the English list, Morley, Balfour, Haldane, Smuts and others. In all of them, Morley least, philosophy has been a major interest, and it is in the philosophical outlook that we find another essential factor in good conversation. It cannot be sustained long on mere facts. The philosophy need not—indeed, should not—be technical, but there must be a philosophical attitude, an ability and willingness to see all round a subject and to trace its implications.

Talk, in fact, should never be exclusively technical, any more than it should deal solely in facts. Talk is to facts much like wine to grapes. They should be there as a foundation, but the aroma and full flavor of a rich Burgundy are far from the individual grapes that were crushed in order that the wine might flow and slowly mature. There is one factor that has played a large part in the de-specializing of talk in Europe, and that is responsible for good talk everywhere, which has been curiously lacking in America—woman. Talk is possibly best between socialized, civilized men, but the process of socializing, civilizing and de-specializing them has been largely the task of woman, a task in which she has signally failed in America.

This topic is complex enough to call for a paper wholly devoted to it, but I think it cannot be denied that woman in America has failed in her age-long duty of civilizing her man. She has merely appropriated leisure and culture to herself. Woman has never made anything of culture without man. As a result of the complete social dichotomy in America, the women have developed an anaemic, uncreative cultural atmosphere, and the social life of both sexes has become uncivilized in a very real sense. A broadly humane culture has suffered in the hands of the women until it has come to be regarded as effeminate dilettantism, and the man, engrossed in his office, shop, study or laboratory, leading his social life by talking shop, whether business, art or profession, to his fellow male workers, has narrowed also into specialism and one-track interests. Yet, on the whole, I think today, in spite of all the Women's Clubs with their papers, the Browning Societies and the rest of the feminine cultural flub-dub, there is more chance for the growth of a genuine cultivated life among the men than among the women of America. Woman having failed to socialize and humanize her man, it may yet be his job to civilize *her*.

I am very far from meaning that good talk must deal with Shakespeare and the musical glasses. What I mean is that good conversation is something quite different from obtaining verbal instruction. We may get an amazing amount of interesting information from a specialist discoursing on his subject, but so can we from the Encyclopaedia Britannica. Good talk affords, perhaps, the best instruction in the world, but it is not the instruction of a text book. A scientist who knew all there was to know about the common house-fly might give us an extremely interesting evening, but if it were solely limited to the objective aspects of this one subject it obviously would not be good conversation in any civilized sense. For that, as we have said, a wide background of knowledge and experience, and a completely de-specialized attitude of mind are required.

There is, perhaps, one other point about American talk that may be noted. There seems to be rather a widespread fear that to indulge in intelligent conversation is to make one's self suspect in a nation of go-getters and he-men. The dominance of business interests and the business type undoubtedly has much to do with this; but tracing it back,

I think we meet the influences of both the frontier and of the American woman again. He-men, of course, are at a premium on the frontier. Moreover, the experience to be derived in a frontier life, if intensive, is extremely narrow. Like a small farm, it may be a good place to start from but it is intellectually killing to remain on it. Not only does the frontier stunt the intellectual life but it makes it suspect. A frontier is essentially democratic, and in all democracies, it is damning to be high-brow. In this respect the influence of the frontier has been deeply felt in American life since the days of Andrew Jackson. But if for this reason good conversation is more or less taboo, so it is for another. By failing to civilize her man and make him a part of any real social life, woman has, as we have said, feminized American culture and conversation to such an extent as to make anything beyond shop-talk appear as effeminate. For this double reason a certain atmosphere has been created in America that is inimical to good talk. There are, of course, many men who can talk well under the right conditions, but the social atmosphere in America all too often does not provide them. Thus Henry Adams, when teaching at Harvard, in spite, as he said, of the "presence of some of the liveliest and most agreeable of men who would have made the joy of London or Paris," found that Cambridge offered only "a social desert that would have starved a polar bear." Even Russell Lowell, William James, the Agassiz's, John Fiske and Francis Child could not make it blossom.

Conversation is distinctly a social art, and it can flourish only where society itself has come to be something of a practised art. It cannot succeed, any more than an orchestra can, with one or two competent players amid a lot of others with no ear for music. One has got to be able to count upon all the members of the group having a certain background and attitude, even when the major interests and occupations of every member of the group are different. For various reasons, the old type of society, in which, from a social point of view, such counting upon could be made with certainty, is breaking down everywhere, but in America the social mixture has always been more heterogeneous than in Europe. I am not speaking in a snobbish sense, any more than it would be snobbish to object to a saxophone and a bass drum taking part in a piece prepared solely for strings. The mental backgrounds, even when there are any that deserve the name, of any ordinarily gathered group of men in America are so different that within their circumscribed spheres they offer but narrow range for talk to wander in. It is continually being brought up against this wall and that. When the right group gets together in America there can be as good talk as anywhere; but it rarely happens, and for the most part even those capable of it have learned to hold their tongues and play safe.

Coming back to what seems to me to be the main point the question mark is likely to continue to be the symbol of the United States so long as its men remain frontiersmen, so long as they continue to devote all their time and strength to subduing a wilderness instead of living in it, whether the wilderness is one of woods and Red Indians or of the stony fields of ever increasing economic wants. If the new land of the High Standard proves to be illimitable, with a frontier retreating further and further ahead of each succeeding generation, the question mark, sign of hungry and empty frontier minds, is not soon to be replaced by civilized conversation. The discussion of an endless succession of things, motors, radios, aeroplanes, or of facts, is not conversation. A full mind, a philosophic outlook, a disinterested interest so to speak, a broad and varied background, are not frontier products. Here and there in America a settler has decided that he will move no further, that he will content himself with the patch he has already cleared, and begin really to live instead of always getting ready to. He has ceased to be a frontiersman and begun to build the next stage of civilization. His talk is apt to be good. Conversation will begin when we cease to expand and begin to concentrate. I read today in a European newspaper that "what Denmark thinks today, Europe thinks tomorrow." Look for little Denmark on the map, and think that over. But, you say, "May I ask . . . ?" Go to!

CHAPTER XI
IS AMERICA YOUNG?

IS AMERICA YOUNG?

I

In 1719 an anonymous New England author who signed himself, rather oddly, "your friend among the Oakes and Pines," gave voice to the doctrine that America was young. Speaking for his day, he said, "The Plow-Man that raiseth Grain is more serviceable to Mankind than the Painter who draws only to please the Eye. . . . The Carpenter who builds a good house to defend us from Wind and Weather is more serviceable than the curious Carver, who employs his Art to please the Fancy." Only, he continues, after further praise of labor, "when a People grow numerous, and part are sufficient to raise necessaries for the whole, then 'tis allowable and laudable, that some should be imployed in innocent Arts more for ornament than Necessity; any innocent business that gets an honest penny, is better than Idleness."

When this anonymous social critic made his comments on the needs of America there was but little more than a fringe of settlement along the Atlantic coast. Boston, with a population of eleven thousand, was about twice as populous as either of its two rivals, Philadelphia and New York. The entire white population of North America was considerably under half a million people. There were scarcely any roads and no public means of transportation. Beyond the scattered coastal settlements, the wilderness stretched three thousand miles to the Pacific. Inhabited by savages and almost interminable in extent, the work of subduing it to the needs of civilized man seemed to call, not for centuries, but for millennia of physical effort.

Owing partly to the indomitable courage and partly to the insatiable greed of the American people, but even more to the inventions of science, what seemed a task for the ages has been accomplished in six generations. On the Pacific coast to-day there are cities as populous as were the greatest in Europe when our New Englander promulgated his doctrine that America was young. Yet that doctrine is as firmly embedded in the popular mind as ever. This is so obvious as hardly to need emphasizing by example, but I may mention what I have noted within a few three days.

When speaking to an American boy of seventeen in regard to certain aspects of American life, he countered immediately with: "But America is young. We are really only about a *hundred and fifty* years old." In the course of conversation only yesterday with an Englishman, the son of one of the great friends America had in England during our Civil War, he said: "Of course you are *young*. We must wait." In a letter just received from a friend at home I find the same idea reiterated. "We are *three hundred* years old," he writes, "England a thousand years old. Will you venture the prophecy that in seven hundred more years, when people have a competency, we shall not educate our sons and daughters for service that does not have immediate economic returns?"

It is worth while to analyze such a persistent and almost universal conception. Just what do we mean when we say that America is young? Has the idea any validity, and what is the effect on the minds of those who so easily use it?

By America, of course, we must mean the American people or the American nation. It is obvious, however, that we cannot use the word nation in this connection in a purely political sense. So rapidly does the loom of history weave that we can now be ranked as among the older nations of western civilization. As an independent and unified nation we long antedate, for example, Italy, which was created only in 1860, or Germany, which was first welded into a nation in 1870, to say nothing of many of even later growth.

II

It is possible that in some minds the idea stems from that popular analogy which would identify a nation or a society with an organism. This analogy, however, like most analogies, is extremely dangerous. It may illuminate certain likenesses between society and a physical organism, but it is not a safe instrument with which to try to discover new likenesses. Because we may fancy that certain functions of society resemble those of an organism, it by no means follows that we can interpret one in terms of the other. In spite of many sociologists and writers on history, like Spengler, there is nothing to prove that a society has its birth, growth, and death in the same way as has a physical organism. Such a metaphor is merely suggestive, and is not only unscientific but may be disastrously misleading. The individual appears in his personal development to repeat the broad stages of our racial development, but I fail to find any law supported by the facts of history indicating that nations infallibly do the same. To force the attempt to make any such law is to glide blindly over such innumerable exceptions as would certainly invalidate any law in scientific thinking. Not only do certain manifestations of cultural life—æsthetic, intellectual, and other—appear in some nations and not in others, but there seems to be no definite sequence in which they appear when they appear at all. We may speak of a human being as young, middle-aged, or old, but such terms lose all meaning when applied to a nation as an organism.

Let us take Greece for example. Was Athens old or young in 450 B.C.? It is not fair to say that she had just reached full maturity because within a half century her architecture flowered in the completion of the Parthenon, her sculpture in the works of Phidias, her poetry in Aeschylus, or her philosophy in Socrates and Plato. That is a mere begging of the question. It is estimating the age by the achievement, whereas, when we say that America is young, we are deferring the possibility of achievement upon the score of age.

How old was England in the age of Elizabeth? How are we to estimate the answer? Are we to date her birth in the period of the savage Britons, the Roman conquest, the Saxon or Norman conquests, or when? Are we to calculate her age by some stage of culture attained, by some infusion of new racial blood, by the formation of a unified language, government, or sense of nationality? How old England was in 1558 when Elizabeth came to the throne is as insoluble as "How old is Ann?" Yet if certain manifestations of culture go with certain national ages, it ought to be easy to date a nation in such a marked phase as the days of Marlowe, Spenser, Shakespeare, Bacon, Byrd, and the whole galaxy of stars of the first magnitude. Nor was the spiritual heaven of that time dotted only with such. One writer tells us that "the young gentleman of Sidney's day was as deft at turning a sonnet as his present-day successor at stopping an approach to the green." Another says that music and song "were not the affair solely of intellectual circles but the creation and inheritance of the whole people." Poetry, music, drama, philosophy, architecture—all the arts, as well as the energy of practical life—were at full flood.

The very first foundation stones were being laid in the building of the British Empire which was to continue to rise and grow until it covers a quarter of the globe. We often hear the period spoken of as gloriously *young*. Was England young or old? If she was young then, was she a baby when the work of building cathedrals was in full swing in the eleventh and twelfth centuries? If she was old and mature in 1600 was she doddering in old age when another great outburst of art and thought came in the years of Victoria? In one sense we may date the birth of England in the age of Elizabeth. It was then that the seed was planted of the great empire that was to be. Of practical activity there was enough, it would seem to absorb the whole energies of any people: wars by sea and land; business being pushed into new quarters of the world in every direction; new commodities being found, new methods of doing business being developed, new trade routes being opened up; attempts at colonizing North and South America; a rebuilding of a large part of the domestic architecture of the whole nation to meet altered conditions of life—all these and other aspects of feverish business activity were evident on every hand. Was it youth, maturity, or old age?

How old, again, is Italy? From one point of view she is

to-day a new nation, throbbing with new life, occupied with
the problems of a "new" country, developing a national
consciousness and her national material resources, as "young"
as America. From another, she was old when Cæsar lay
in his blood. I have recently been in Czechoslovakia. As
a political nation she is only ten years old. As I passed
through her villages on the way from Dresden, they looked
newer than Kansas, the whole countryside having been
rebuilt while the peasants were afraid to put their money into
anything but building on account of the steady fall in the
currency. In Prague I was told that the nation was new,
that the task of building it would absorb all the energies of
its people, that the work of developing its resources was
overwhelming, that for the present it "did not want learned
men, artists, or writers, but business men, engineers, practical
men. Later," my informant continued,"the rest may come,
but not now." It was the New England voice "from the
Oakes and Pines" of 1719. Yet here and there one saw on
hilltops castles ten centuries old. In the fields one saw men
in the furrows following yoked white oxen as in the days of
Virgil. Is Czechoslovakia young or, from the standpoint of
America, very, very old?

Does age mean the accumulation of resources from the
past—old buildings, cathedrals, picture galleries, and all the
valuable opportunities to see and to study? All these
doubtless help, but how much of all such did the common
people of Athens have when they crowded as multitudinously
to hear the plays of Æschylus, Sophocles and Euripides as
the modern *hoi polloi* of America crowd to see the latest sex
film on the screen? In 1787 we were nearly a century and a
half "younger" than we are now, but if we held a constitu-

tional convention in 1930 should we be able to send any better thinkers or more broadly cultured men than those who drew up our first constitution? Would the discussion and propaganda regarding a political problem to-day show any advance in maturity and power of thought on the part of both writers and readers over the papers of the *Federalist?* It may well be that not only an outburst of art and literature, such as has happened now and again in the world's history, but the degree of a cultured civilization to which a nation as, say the French, comes to attain, have no ascertainable cause, that they come from combinations deep in human nature too inscrutable to be observed or predicted. That is probably the case, but if so why claim that they are the products or accompaniments of a given age, and that we cannot expect them before a certain period any more than in the human body we can look for puberty or the growth of a beard or the coming of the wisdom teeth?

This question of national age becomes more puzzling the more we think about it, but in trying to solve it let us turn to America, the land that everyone says is young. We may, as we have seen, dismiss at once, I think, certain interpretations of age. We may discard the thought of any analogy with an organism. We can date a human being as five, fourteen, twenty-one, or three score and ten years of age, and have it mean something. We cannot date a nation as one century, five, or twenty, and have it mean anything with scientific accuracy. Again, we may discard the thought of independence or political nationhood. My young friend, probably taught by his elders, evidently had that point in mind. Arguing that way, we should be a century older than

Italy or Germany, but those who argue that America is young would not accept that conclusion.

We have got, again, to dismiss as a criterion the stage of culture which a people has arrived at—the arts, inventions, knowledge which they have inherited from the past. Every settler who came to America had behind him all the past just as much as did his family or neighbors who remained behind. The seventeenth-century English, Scotch, Germans, Swedes, Dutch, and others who came here in our first century were not barbarians. They had the entire inheritance from the past. They were heirs of Greece and Rome, of the Reformation and the Renaissance, as much as those who continued in the old countries; and every man who has come here since has been of the same national age as those he has left behind.

III

In analyzing this idea of our being a young nation, I cannot see that there is any valid way in which to date ourselves as compared with others, and I believe that the constant insisting upon this misleading way of putting the truth (for there *is* a truth about our case which I shall elaborate in a moment) is beginning to do us deep hurt. I believe that it would be far better for the development of our best selves, individually and nationally, if instead of consistently thinking and speaking of the American people as "young," we should think and say the clear truth, which is that we are an old people, the same age as our European cousins, who *moved into an unsettled world.* Not only is the content of these two ideas very different, but so also are the inferences often very loosely and carelessly drawn from them.

The moving into a new country was bound to have important consequences. Even the moving of a family into a new house usually marks a change. The mere move itself is apt to bring about a feeling of excitement and exhilaration if the move is for the better, or depression and sorrow if it is for the worse. For a while after the move, also, there is much to be done of a purely physical sort. One has to rearrange one's furniture, get "shaken down," as we say; perhaps do all sorts of things to house and garden; get used to a new neighborhood; find new shops; learn new ways of doing old things; in a word, the whole routine of daily life is altered for the time being, and our habits and the enjoyment of our tastes are apt to be broken in upon until we get over the pressing work of settling into the new place.

In moving into America there was much more involved, mentally and physically, than in such a move as we have just described. Not only was the break with the old home and the old associations more complete, but everything, literally, from the ground up had to be done in the new. The savages had to be fought; the land had to be cleared; the houses had to be constructed; a new life, socially and institutionally, had to be built up. I have pointed out elsewhere the effect of this on the minds of the settlers. It is also, of course, a fact of great significance for American cultural life that, speaking comparatively, almost without exception all the immigrants who have ever come here have been men of the lower middle and laboring classes. There was nothing in America to attract any of the wealthy or professional ones. With the exception of a few religious refugees, virtually all who have come here have been "practical" men, who have come to better their economic positions. They did not include in their numbers aristocrats, scholars, poets, dramatists, artists, any of the classes who were carrying on and developing the European cultural tradition. But in some respects the arts were more diffused in their practice and enjoyment among the lower classes in the Europe from which our earlier settlers came than they are to-day. Many brought books and many a love and taste for music and the various handicrafts, such as weaving, woodcarving of houses and furniture, and other things, no less truly arts because they were folk-arts.

The effort, however, to establish a European standard of living in the wilderness was too great. The intellectual and æsthetic enjoyments of life had to be laid aside until the practical duties of subduing the wilderness had been fulfilled. All this is well enough understood. But let us suppose for a moment that the North American continent had consisted of that strip of land between the ocean and the Appalachian range of mountains, beyond which we will place the Pacific. By 1776 practically all of this territory was settled as peacefully as was England itself. In fact, much of it looked like England. Boston was to all intents and purposes identical with an English provincial town. Travelers reported that much of the New England countryside was indistinguishable from that of old England. Wealth had accumulated; colleges had been erected; the arts were beginning to flourish. In the 1750's the theater in New York offered a better repertoire than could be found in any English provincial city of the time, and I am not sure but as good as that of London itself, certainly better than can be heard some years in New York now. Mr. and Mrs. Hallam, actors of note in London, arrived in the colonies with their company

and remained twenty years. They acted in plays of Shakespeare, Addison, Rowe, Congreve, Farquhar, Steele, and
others; and in 1754 New York had a season in which twenty-
one different plays, the cream of English dramatic literature
up to that time, were heard by the public. Such plays were
also given in such a surprising list of places as Philadelphia,
Williamsburg, Annapolis, Hobb's Hole, Port Tobacco,
Upper Marlborough, Petersburg, and Fredericksburg. The
theatrical and musical life of Charleston could hardly have
been excelled, if it was, in any provincial town in England.

In 1757 the first exhibition of paintings by colonial artisst
was held in New York. Before long, Copley, Peale, Benjamin
West, who later became president of the Royal Academy,
and Stuart were painting and, with lesser figures, were
in the way of establishing an American school of art. Colonial
architecture, domestic and public, was so good that we do
our best to reproduce it to-day, as was likewise the furniture.
Merchants in the North, country gentlemen in the South,
lived much the same lives as did their contemporaries of
similar standing in the old country. The ablest men of the
colonies in innumeragle instances held legislative and judicial
offices. There was no titled aristocracy, there were no
cathedrals or ruined castles from the past, life was a little
freer, less formal, considerably more open to economic
opportunity than in England; but so far from excusing
themselves on the ground of being a new people the colonials
rather prided themselves on living the same life and indulging
the same tastes as their cousins overseas. America was
indeed provincial, but then, so also was all England outside
the one center of London. Much not only of the talent but
the genius of England had always been recruited from the

provinces, and America had made a good beginning two centuries ago in contributing, among other types, men whose paintings hang to-day on the walls of London galleries. Franklin's fame was European. When Berkeley, the English philosopher, was temporarily living in Rhode Island he found no lack of agreeable society and intelligent conversation in the circle in which he moved. The lower grades had permanently lost their folk-arts and had taken on some frontier characteristics, but there was every indication that a new civilization, following the main cultural interests, values, and trends of the old, was arising rapidly after the break due to the task of subduing the wilderness. Had the continent been limited, as I suggested, to the seaboard strip, or had the people chosen to expand gradually, there is no reason to suppose that the cultural tendencies noted above as on the upward trend through the eighteenth century would not have continued.

The continent, however, was not so limited. It stretched nearly three thousand miles further. It was incredibly rich. Following the Revolution, piece after piece of it, at intervals, came into the hands of the descendants of those eighteenth-century colonials, men quite as much as women, who had begun to interest themselves in painting, literature, drama, and music. The wealth to be made out of the West, a constantly retreating West for more than a century, began to act as a magnet on men's minds and ambitions. Following the poorer classes who went as hunters and settlers, there appear the agents of merchants, bankers, and speculators. Astor made a fortune in furs. Others in lands. Others in yet more ways. The craze for getting fabulously rich quickly spread. The perpetual boom, broken only by sharp crises, in which America has since lived, began. The nascent civilization on the seaboard became violently deflected from its course. Scientific inventions succeeded one another, and with every new method of transportation—canal, good roads, steamboat, railroad—every new method of mining, every new product to be utilized, every new foreign market opened, the rush to win riches by raping a continent became madder and madder.

It was not a question of preparing a continent for habitation. It was one of money-maddened men furiously wrenching wealth from it in every way their ingenuity and greed could devise—from the land, from the forests above it, from the mines below it. Like hogs at a trough, each man guzzled as hard as he could, regardless of all else, lest some other hog should get ahead of him. In Germany they have been rafting logs for a thousand years. The carefully tended and replanted forests may well last for a thousand more. Rafting on the Mississippi began, flourished, and was finished in seventy years. About 1840 the American people as a nation owned forty billion feet of standing lumber contiguous to the river and its tributaries. In seventy years private individuals and companies had stripped the land of this magnificent heritage without replacing a single tree. This was not "the task of subduing a wilderness to make it habitable." It was the madness of lust—the meanest of all lusts, the lust for money.

To-day America is fairly glutted with wealth. It is useless to enumerate the statistics—an advertising expenditure of a billion dollars a year, savings deposits of twenty-eight billions, two hundred and twenty-eight individuals reporting incomes of over a million a year each, a national income of ninety billions.

IV

Is America still young? Is it not rather, perhaps, if we *must* use such figures of speech, that she was born at Jamestown in 1607, grew to promising maturity by the second half of the eighteenth century, and then, abandoning herself to the desire for expansion and sudden wealth, deliberately turned her back on the way in which she had been going? Those who say that America is young, still point to the future as the time when we may be expected to begin to devote ourselves to other things than "subduing a continent and accumulating the necessary material resources on which to build a civilization." In the name of every high ideal that man has ever cherished, *when* are we going to be rich enough to begin as a nation, if we are not now, now that we have gutted our heritage, piled up the greatest accumulation of wealth in the world, accumulated the most stupendous material basis for living that man has ever known?

I think it is at this point that the dangerous evil of our being forever told by friendly or hostile critics that we are young comes in. A boy who is really young realizes that there are some things he cannot do until he is a man. He waits, but at the same time he prepares himself. If we tell a child he is too young to do this or that, the child is justified in believing it and in refraining from trying to do it. Is there not danger in telling our people, young and old, that America is young? Will it not merely serve to make them contented to go on piling up wealth, to do what they have been doing for a hundred years, and to keep them from playing the part of men as they should? Many critics have pointed to the immaturity of the American mind.

There is a time to stop telling a boy he is young. There comes a time when we must tell him to be a man, to do a man's work and try to think a man's thoughts. If we keep on coddling him and telling him he is a child of whom nothing is expected, we are not likely ever to make a man of him.

Why should we be content to wait a hundred, two hundred, or seven hundred years more before we think we shall be old enough to do something besides provide the material foundation for a civilization which we are told will somehow come of itself when we are grown up? If we are told and come to believe that no matter what we do we cannot lead a more spiritual life or have the culture of an "old" country in less than so many centuries, any more than a boy of fourteen can make himself twenty by trying, are we not giving ourselves an excuse to go on piling up riches and exploiting the world without making an effort to attain to a spiritual instead of a material plane of civilization?

On the other hand, if we think of ourselves as an old race, heirs of all the ages, which was temporarily set back by having to move into a new home, and that now we have not only got that home in order but have added to it and become incredibly rich, and that therefore it is high time we turned to something else, I believe it would be far better for our self-respect and for our spiritual growth. To say that we are too young is to put off the time of manhood beyond our power to attain, and to stultify any hopes of our own day and generation. To say, on the other hand, that we have made our move, got settled, and become rich is to stir us to something better than spending our days devising more means to get richer yet.

[255]

I do not believe we *are* young. We are a century and a half older than when a political gathering could include such minds as John Adams, Franklin, Jefferson, Hamilton, John Marshall, and others. We are nearly a century older than when in one corner of our land alone we could have a group like Holmes, Whittier, Hawthorne, Lowell, and Emerson. I believe in many ways we have already added much to the spiritual wealth of the world. In our library systems, in our scientific foundations for research, in a number of other ways, we have led the modern nations. Why, then, still preach this debilitating doctrine that we are young and nothing must be expected of us? Is it not time that we stopped using that as an excuse to cover all our shortcomings, the desire not to stop hunting after material gain, the refusal to stir our minds and play a man's part in the new world? Is it not time to proclaim that we are not children but men who must put away childish things; that we have overlooked that fact too long; that we have busied ourselves overmuch with fixing up the new place we moved into three hundred years ago, with making money in the new neighborhood; and that we should begin to live a sane, maturely civilized life? To keep on telling our children that they cannot expect this and that of America because she is too young is to make self-indulgent, self-excusing mollycoddles of them and of her. To say that we cannot yet turn to the spiritual things of life because we still have material work to do, when we contrast our own gorged state of material well-being with that of any other nation, is sheer hypocrisy. If we merely want to continue to grow richer and richer, and softer and softer, let us say so straight out and not hide the truth under the plea of having to "develop the continent," that contiment which Jefferson fondly hoped would leave us room for expansion for a thousand years. Everything may be hoped from the child who tries to be a man. Nothing can be hoped from the man who cloaks his shortcomings or material selfishness or spiritual indolence under the pretense of being a child.

CHAPTER XII
HOME THOUGHTS FROM ABROAD

HOME THOUGHTS FROM ABROAD

I

After some months at "home" in America and a couple
spent in rambling over Italy and France, I returned recently once more to London. The first thing that struck
me, happily, was that its perennial and inexhaustible
charm was as fresh and unchanged as ever. It is true that
changes in detail, mainly architectural, are to be observed
as plentiful enough by one who has long known it and who
has now been an annual visitor for some years. Devonshire
House, never a thing of beauty, but nevertheless of a certain
antique dignity, has given place to a glaringly white palace of
smart flats and shops. The yet newer but equally glaring
hotel in Park Lane is regarded with many shakings of heads
as a possible portent for what may be in store for the entire
length of that aristocratic street. Dorchester House, most
beautiful of all the great houses in town, has been sold in
spite of efforts to save it from the auctioneer's hammer and
probable destruction. Burlington Arcade, beloved of all
shopping tourists, has also changed hands and its fate is
unknown. The Adelphi, with its dignified houses above and
its gloomy and mysterious "arches" below ,is about to be
disposed of. The dark passageways, lit at midday by flaring
gas lamps, and housing, besides memories of David Copper-
field, the largest and perhaps choicest collections of wines
in the world, are probably doomed. I hesitate to say too

much about it for American readers, but there are estimated to be between three and four hundred thousand dozen of priceless vintages stored in the vaults which will soon have to be moved. At least, although the fate of the buildings still hangs in the balance, Bernard Shaw, who has lived there for thirty years, has taken, with Celtic impatience, a flat elsewhere, and Sir James Barrie, another tenant, is, with more British calm, "waiting," as he says, "to see." As for the complete transformation of lower Regent Street, in progress for several years, the alterations are now practically completed and the new buildings will require many months of damp and soot to mellow into harmonious tone with their surroundings.

Yes, in some external features London is undoubtedly changing, and changing rapidly. But then, it always has been changing since it was founded by the Romans nearly two thousand years ago. Here and there we may lament some particular manifestation of the law of life and growth, but as a whole one finds the life of the town singularly unaltered, and London still seems to me in most ways the most civilized, as it is unquestionably the greatest, of the cities of men.

Coming from the Continent, a "citizen of the world" feels at once that he has come from the backwaters into a great centre of human interest. London is not only in sheer extent and population the largest city in the world, so that Paris, and even New York in the restricted limits of its only interesting portions, seem quickly exhaustible in comparison, but it is the centre as yet of the greatest and most widely scattered empire the world has ever seen. The dweller in it feels that he is at the crossroads of all the world's chief highways. One can survey the world from here as from no other one centre. France, it is true, has a scattered empire also, but the average Frenchman has, for the most part, as little interest in the world at large as has the American of the Middle West. Italy's empire and interests are almost wholly confined to the shores of the Mediterranean, to say nothing of the iron censorship of speech and press. Except for international sport and the spectacular, the average city in America is as unconscious of what is being said and done in other countries as is a man of the radio waves carried on the ether. By "listening in" he may at once pick up a whole world of sound and thought of which he is otherwise unconscious. In the same way a man at home may "listen in" to the international world by using special apparatus in the way of foreign journals or by personal relations, but these opportunities are limited to comparatively small groups.

Here, on the other hand, that world is, so to say, in the air and not the ether, and one does not have to make a special effort or acquire exceptional apparatus to share in it. There are certain types of the stay-at-home smaller business Englishman who are as hopelessly narrow and provincial as Babbitt. But, even if one is not a Joshua to fell the walls of high society or the higher political circles, one is more apt here to meet all the time people who have just come from China or the Cape, or almost any part of the world, than one is at home to meet strayers from Dayton or Houston or Los Angeles. Moreover, if one picks up a dozen English magazines on the news stand and contrasts them with a dozen American ones, the wider range of interests at once becomes apparent. Of course, there are reasons for this. The main business of England, both in merchandising and banking, is international. The larger business man has a direct interest in almost all quarters of the globe. Again, speaking broadly, there is scarcely a family of the better-magazine-reading classes which has not a member of it living in some remote corner of the Empire or of the world outside. Cape Town, Calcutta, and Peking are not merely far-off foreign cities which creep into the news occasionally as centres of political disturbance, but places where "Tom" or "Dick" or "Harry" is stationed.

But another and perhaps one of the chief charms of London is that, if it is the greatest of all great cities, it is also the most homelike and, one might almost say, rural. The low sky line, and the fact that the architectural unit for most of the town yet remains the small house as contrasted with the vast "apartment houses" and skyscrapers of American cities, account for part of this "homey" atmosphere for a generation which still feels that a home means a house and not a slice of some costly communal barracks. Then there are the parks everywhere, affording not only the welcome relief of lawns and trees, but opportunities for cricket and golf and tennis within walking distance of one's house almost wherever it may be. Apart from the innumerable larger parks there are the endless "squares" and "gardens," so that one may walk in almost any direction not more than a few minutes without the eye's encountering the restful green of trees and shrubs. Cheek by jowl with the busiest thoroughfares there are village-seeming streets or quiet nooks which are as retired and peace-bringing as any cathedral close. One steps out of Piccadilly to find one's self surrounded by the flowers and country atmosphere of the Albany, or one passes from the confusion of High Holborn under an archway to rest in the charming old-world garden of Staple Inn, where the lilacs and iris bloom and a fountain plashes with the cool serenity of the garden sanctuary of some country house. Again, one may pass from the Strand, busiest of the streets of men, under another archway to the perfect sylvan peace of the Temple, where lawns stretch to the river and boys and girls are playing tennis and one feels a brooding calm under the shade of almost immemorial trees. One of the loveliest rural views in England is looking up the water in St. James Park, only three minutes from what, with the Abbey and Parliament Buildings, may be called the very centre of Empire. Starting there, one may walk for miles over grass and under the trees, keeping all the time in the heart of London. I know in America no country club to compare in sheer rural beauty with Ranelagh, with its superb gardens, its flowers, water views, tennis courts, golf course, and polo grounds, yet this, like Hurlingham, is not an hour or so out of town by train, but on one of the busiest arteries of traffic within the city itself.

All these open spaces, all this green and the scent of flowers, give one the impression that everywhere the country is overflowing into the city. One hears the syrinx rather than the riveter, and Pan and Flora yet hold the field against Midas and Vulcan. Nowhere in London, with the exception of the Mall and perhaps one or two other instances, do we find any such planned architectural vistas as so delight the French. London, vast as a primeval forest, has just naturally grown without elaborate city planning, but unlike New York and the larger American cities it has managed to keep itself green and homelike and beautiful. Nature has not been banished, but welcomed in a thousand nooks and corners prepared for her to enter. The difference seems to depend on national taste and a different scale of values. In America the sole "value" of a piece of city real estate is considered to be what it will yield when built upon, and every inch is made to produce as much as possible by building on it. Here —although, Heaven knows, London land is costly enough— open spaces, irises and daffodils, hawthorns and lawns, have their values also for the human life of the town. The Bank of England is at present erecting a huge new building for its needs, but it is being so constructed as to preserve the small patch of shaded green where daffodils bloom in gay disregard of the swirling traffic a few feet away in one of the most congested centers of the world. Imagine a great bank in Wall Street having a garden! Anyone who suggested it would be thought mad, but in London it is this sense of human values, in private properties as well as public parks, maintained in spite of the need and lure of money in the world's most densely populated city, which again gives one a sense of its civilized attitude toward life.

Yet another element in its civilization is the almost perfect quiet that reigns in it. As contrasted with the insane tooting of horns day and night in Paris and New York, one rarely hears a motor, and although these warm days the parks are filled with children and older persons of all grades of society, walking about or playing games, one never hears any such "catcalling," yelling, and general racket as one would in American city parks with such masses of people. Civilization is of necessity a colossal compromise between impulses of self-expression in an individual and his strength of will in controlling such impulses as, indulged in by many others, would make life less possible or agreeable for all. When one motorist, dashing through a street at night, gives vent to his self-expression by a shriek of his horn which awakens with a start perhaps a hundred people, he is a being who has not learned the very rudiments of civilization—that is, of harmonizing his own instincts with the good of all.

Perhaps the highest test of whether a city or a people is civilized is just this one of how far it has gone in learning what things can and cannot be done in order to attain to the most perfect balance between expression and restraint. This, of course, is most obviously manifested in the nature and character of the laws, in the speed and impartiality with which they are enforced, and in the attitude of the people at large to them. One feels here that, whether by centuries of training or by some political instinct, this people can govern itself as no other can. There are comparatively few laws interfering with the liberty of the individual to do as he likes, but they are enforced with a swiftness, an impartiality, and a completeness that leave an American green with envy. To note merely two examples since my arrival: About three weeks ago a woman's body was found in a trunk which had been checked at Charing Cross Station. There was no apparent clue to the mystery. At the end of a week the newspapers were much perturbed by what they called the "unique" and most disturbing fact that after seven days the police had not yet caught the unknown murderer. A few days later, however, he had been run down, had confessed, and is now in jail. Shortly after this a most outrageous blackmailing scheme was brought to the attention of the police. Within a fortnight the ringleaders had been caught,

[267]

tried, convicted, and sent to prison for terms ranging up
to life.

It may be said that good enforcement of the law might
also be had under an autocracy, but what strikes one here
as a test of civilization is not merely the enforcement of law
by the authorities, but the attitude of the people themselves
toward it in a democracy. Take the case of the regulation
of the liquor traffic. We tried it ourselves at home for years;
but, on the one hand, the authorities proved themselves too
incompetent and venal to enforce any laws regulating the
saloon, and, on the other, the people as a whole were too
lawless to make the problem a small one. From this we
went on to Prohibition, with the resulting farcical but no
less disgraceful mess we are in to-day. Over here, ever since
the war, the traffic has been regulated by permitting sales
only at certain hours of the day, and it is illuminating to see
how the law is everywhere enforced by the people themselves.
The hours vary slightly in different towns so that not infrequently in the past five years I have found myself asking
for a drink in a public house or hotel a few minutes ahead of
the particular opening time in that locality. In all these
years I have never yet witnessed a single case in which the
law has been infringed by the fraction of a second on my
behalf or that of anyone else. As a result, the law has been
entirely successful. The possibility of prohibition, with all
its evils, has been put off indefinitely, and on the other hand
drunkenness has ceased, as far as my observation has gone.
I have seen only one case of even semi-intoxication, that of
a man who had that afternoon received a decree of divorce
and was either drowning his sorrows or celebrating his luck,
I never knew which. Over the Whitsuntide holiday, I might

add, some two hundred and fifty thousand persons went to Blackpool, and there was not a single instance of drunkenness or disorderly conduct.

II

Certainly if we judge the degree of civilization by the completeness with which a people governs itself, combined with the completeness with which it retains all possible liberty of individual action, I know no other leading country of European civilization which can compete with England. As for liberty of speech, thought, and action in America, it is notorious that in many ways they are being maintained only by a direct disobeying of or winking at innumerable laws.

To some extent we may attribute some of our difficulties of this sort to the extremely heterogeneous population we now have, but that is due to the "native" American's dislike of physical work and his desire to get rich as quickly as possible by exploiting with the greatest speed and with alien labor the resources of the continent. At home there is no use blinking the fact any longer that we are not an Anglo-Saxon country. Our language may be English, the framework of our government may be mainly derived from English precedents, and the old stock may still give the leaders, for the most part, in culture, but the population figures tell another story. In New York City alone there are two million foreign born and two hundred thousand negroes, to say nothing of foreigners of the second generation. In all England there are only three hundred thousand aliens, and this racial solidarity gives one a sense of being at home and among one's own kind.

The figures in *Who's Who* are suggestive. That volume is supposed to list some twenty-six thousand Americans who have achieved enough distinction to win a place there. Of those twenty-six thousand, as I recall it, ten per cent were foreign born, but of that ten per cent one half came to us from the British Empire, leaving only five per cent, or some thirteen hundred persons in all America, who have achieved distinction from among the millions of all other races who have been immigrants in the last generation. For the most part, we get the lowest and not the best from foreign countries, and, apart from a few notable individuals, their purely cultural contribution to American life has been small. The types of civilization evolved by various races all have their good and bad points, but each has been fitted to racial idiosyncrasies. The world would be poorer without either the Anglo-Saxon or the Latin; but, to mention only one point, when we study what the Latins have everywhere made of parliamentary government of the English type it is evident that it is utterly unsuited to them. It is not one of the least satisfactions of living in England that one is surrounded by English people. In America one is also surrounded by "Americans," but "American" has utterly ceased to have any racial connotation. In the colonial days, in spite of a considerable admixture of Germans, Dutch, Scotch, and Irish, the social fabric was still English, and it is not surprising if an American of English descent whose family had been in America for many generations before the separation took place should still prefer an English attitude and outlook on life to that of the Semites or Slavs or Armenians, however interesting he may find certain aspects of their self-expression in literature or art.

I have mentioned the charm of the flowers in London, but the children, dainty and flowerlike, are no less charming, and these warm days the parks and squares and streets are full of them. As great numbers of the boys of the better classes are away at school, the girls are most in evidence, with their skirts so short as to be mere flounces on the bottom of abbreviated waists. One can study childish legs from ankle to hip here by the thousand, and one comes to the conclusion that they are among the most beautiful things the world has to offer. These youngsters, arrayed in a way to make Main Street gasp, have also a gentleness, a modesty, and a quietness of demeanor that are equally beyond the ken of that thoroughfare.

One could continue to write indefinitely of the charms of London, but already many readers have undoubtedly been giving vent to that characteristic remark whenever one praises foreign lands or suggests anything lacking in "God's Country": "Why don't you go there to live if you think it's so much better?"—with an inflection of annoyance that makes the sentence much more of an imperative than an interrogative. Over here, year after year, as one's life passes so easily and humanely, one asks one's self that question, especially as one reads that marvelously fascinating last page of the morning *Times* with its illustrated advertisements, veritable "magic casements," of country houses for sale at fabulously low prices according to American standards. Also one knows one can be sure of a cook. Why not stay here and live? And yet one doesn't—or, at least, one has not yet.

As for the mere matter of changing one's residence, American opinion has always been irrational. Americans think it laudable that a citizen of any other nation should

come to America to better his condition, but shameful that
an American should emigrate to Europe for the same purpose.
Let an Astor or a Henry James or an Edwin Abbey transfer
himself to England and, in the American vernacular, "a
howl goes up" as though he had been a Benedict Arnold.
But life after all is not rational, and one hesitates. The advantages of this country are all rational. The reasons for
not packing up forthwith are largely irrational and usually
they win, though they are not easy to describe.

There is at bottom that largely modern and perhaps hard-
est of all passions to analyze, the love of one's country, even
in America where in many neighborhoods one's neighbors
have ceased to be of one's own race or even, perhaps, capable
of speaking one's own tongue. As one looks at the beautiful
English landscape, more beautiful in its well-tended charm
and utter peacefulness than any other I know in the whole
world, a sudden nostalgia will come over one for a rough,
neglected bit of some Vermont hillside or the familiar ugliness
of some fishing village on the shore. One murmurs to one's
self, "Beautiful, beautiful," in Devon or Warwickshire, and
then may unaccountably be seized with a sudden desire to
"muss it all up." All Englishmen have to some extent this
love of the wild and the unfinished, and perhaps those of us
whose families have been in America for centuries—and
mine, counting South as well as North America, was here for
two generations before even the Mayflower sailed—have
"gone native" a bit, have become a little more uncivilized, a
little savage. Something revolts in us at living too contin-
uously too perfect, too orderly, too civilized a life.

Perhaps the scale has something to do with it. Mere big-
ness, so much worshiped at home, has no value in itself.

Many a tiny insect is more beautiful than an elephant. But there is a sense in which size when translated into scale has a legitimate influence. A miniature, an easel painting, and a mural decoration differ in something more than mere size. So far as I know, no attempt has been made to study the effect of the size of a man's habitation upon him, though as the average man's grows smaller and smaller it is a subject not without interest. What are all the psychological effects of living in two rooms and a bath as compared with the old roomy house of two generations ago? Over here one feels at times that sense of being "cabin'd, cribb'd, confin'd." One recalls the picture in *Punch* of an American motorist driving his car at seventy miles an hour while a man by the roadside calls out, "Remember this is an island!" Even if one has lived only on the Atlantic seaboard, he has felt that there were three thousand miles of open sea in front of him and three thousand miles of his own land behind him, and it has done something, very lasting but very hard to define, to him.

But perhaps most of all there is the feeling that at home one is watching one of the greatest experiments in history, an experiment that is somehow partly one's own responsibility as an American. If one loses one's way in the subway because the conductor can talk only Hungarian, if some negroes are burned at the stake as though it were the year 800, if a bricklayer gets twenty dollars a day and a professor of economics gets ten, if a town can find no better way to express its enthusiasm for a native son than by running the fire engines up and down the main street, if twenty thousand school children are assembled to see which has the most freckles, if any one of the hundred unaccountable and fantastic things in the American press come true daily, one wonders what it all signifies and where it is all going to end. But that is just it. One wonders and one wants to wait just a little longer and see. Perhaps the small boy has never lost his love for the circus.

III

In speaking with American friends at home I find that there is a widespread opinion that the English do not like us and that a tourist or resident here is acutely made aware of the fact. I have spent part of each of the last six years in England and have found very little of this alleged hostility to ourselves.

There is no other human relationship more apt to breed bad blood and misunderstanding than that between debtor and creditor, as the entire history of our country proves in the relations between East and West. The trouble is apt to be greatly emphasized when such a relation is suddenly reversed and the formerly rich creditor finds himself in turn in the rôle of poor debtor. The debt of the now comparatively poor England to the enormously prosperous America might well have been expected to have bred ill feeling of the deepest sort, but it has not done so to anything like the degree which it has on the continent of Europe. In the first place, there has been the long-ingrained respect in England for business ethics. She has been called a nation of shop-keepers, but the very conditions that have called forth that name have bred in her a sense of commercial honor that is notably lacking in certain other countries. The war debt has therefore been regarded here much more than in any other debtor country in the same light in which the business man in

America has regarded it—that is, as a purely financial transaction the terms of which should be complied with as far as possible. Also the English are good sports and believe in "playing cricket."

It is true that England would have been glad to see all debts canceled for the good of all, and in this she was not as selfish as has been claimed, for the debts owing her by other nations are much more than she owes and she would have lost heavily on balance by such an all-round cancellation. This balance she has, as a matter of fact, relinquished by canceling all debts due her except enough to pay us, provided she can collect it, which is not by any means yet certain. English business, including manufactures, commerce, and banking, has always been international, whereas American has been almost wholly domestic. The average American has little or nothing to do with the complicated problems of foreign exchange, and the English can see far more clearly the future difficulties involved for the entire business of the world in these enormous annual payments by Europe to a country which already has half the world's gold supply. The task of paying international debts raises problems which are entirely different from the mere transfer of domestic credits, and the securing of funds to be transferred annually to America is far from being solely a matter of taxation, however staggering. When, in addition to insisting that the debts be paid to the uttermost farthing possible, according to our standard of the debtors' "capacity to pay," we raise a tariff wall which prohibits the sale of foreign goods to us, an almost impossible situation is created. We already have the gold, so they cannot pay us in that. We refuse to let them pay us in goods.

We prohibit the import of wool, for example, one of England's chief exports, by raising the duty to sixty per cent. As a personal experience, last year on the dock I found the duty on my suits to be the figure just named, on embroidery seventy-five per cent, on jewelry eighty per cent, and on lace ninety per cent. In the old days we used to imprison debtors who could not pay. We gradually learned that shutting a man in jail and depriving him of the means of making a livelihood was a foolish way to expect him to pay his debt. By our tariff wall we are imprisoning our European debtors in much the same way. This phase of the problem is resented to some extent here because the situation is much better understood than at home, where most business men have had experience only with domestic debts, with no training in international finance.

On the whole, however, one hears comparatively little here now about the debt. In responsible quarters there is a great desire to let the matter rest and to continue to make the annual payments without further comment unless the ultimate impossibility of the situation may become clearly apparent on both sides of the water. It does hurt and annoy them here when Mr. Mellon tells the American people that the debt is not costing England anything and is not hurting her. If Englishmen are not given either to whimpering or to welshing, they do believe in fair play. They may or may not eventually receive from other nations what they are already paying us. They have not received it yet, and may never do so. They are engaged in delicate negotiations with France about the matter now. Meanwhile they have signed the note to us and are paying it in cash. Therefore, when they are bleeding themselves white in their private and corporate incomes to pay their own taxes (the lowest income-tax rate is twenty per cent), and are paying the debt to us on a scale which we have not exacted from any other debtor, they feel it is unfair to say they are not going into their own pockets at all. But even so, there was much criticism here of Churchill's note as tending to start afresh a controversy which Englishmen feel is settled and which it is beneath their dignity to reopen of themselves.

Among people of all classes I would say that there is far less feeling against the United States here than there is against England even now at home, with all the improvement that there has been in sentiment there. Perhaps the most absurd opinion which many people in the smaller communities in America hold is that England hates us because she has never forgotten the Revolution. As for the loss of a major part of her earlier empire, several points must be remembered which Americans are apt to forget. One is that for many decades in the nineteenth century public opinion in England was not imperialistic at all, and, so far from regretting the loss of the United States, the country was in favor of divesting itself as soon as possible of the rest of its imperial possessions. The imperialism of to-day is of comparatively recent growth, with a long interval of anti-imperial feeling between the loss of the old empire and the present day. Again, England has no grievance or rankling soreness from being defeated by Americans. There is a simple reason for this, usually ignored at home. It is that she never was so defeated. She was beaten not by her colonies, but by a coalition of European Powers that came to their aid. Washington admitted that the game was lost and that the only salvation was to have France, at least, enter the fight. Not only did France do so, but Spain also, and England was fighting all over the world as well as in America, and continued to do so a year and more after Cornwallis surrendered. She was beaten only by the combined power of nearly half the civilized world.

As a matter of fact, the Pilgrim Fathers, the Revolution, and all the rest of our history, so familiar either in fact or legend to American children, are to a great extent not known at all here. It was only about four years ago that the first chair of American history in any English university was founded. The cultural contributions of America to civilization had been comparatively slight, and until we became a world power, owing to our wealth and numbers, there was little more reason for Europe's being interested in our history than there is for us to study the local historical details of South Africa or Australia. The situation is well illustrated by a story which I heard Lord Lee of Fareham, who has an American wife, tell the other day. She thought she would make a pious pilgrimage to Plymouth to see the place from which her ancestors had sailed. Trying to find the dock,—where, by the way, there is a commemorative tablet,—she asked a man if he could tell her where the Pilgrims had sailed from. He looked puzzled and finally replied: "I really do not recall them, madam. Did they sail recently?" The Standard Life Assurance Company is at present running a series of advertisements in one of the best-known English weeklies using "historical incidents" as texts. Last week they inserted one on the sailing of the Mayflower. Explaining briefly for English readers who the Pilgrim Fathers were, the notice says that "after a short stay in Holland they sailed for America, where they founded a colony at New Plymouth in 1621" [sic]. This is evidently all new and requiring explanation to English people, although any American child could point out the several errors of fact in that one sentence.

Far from discovering any feeling of antagonism here on the score of history, an American is constantly amazed to find how the greater men on either side of the ocean are considered to belong to one common race. It would be a delicate if not an impossible matter to set up the statue of an English king in America, though Alfred and Edward and all the others down to George the Third are as much figures in our history as in England's. It would also be difficult to erect the statue of any great Englishman of recent days. But here one is becoming surrounded with Americans. If one goes into the crypt of St. Paul's Cathedral one finds a bust of Washington gazing at the tomb of Nelson, and there are many tablets there commemorating American artists. I was surprised by finding one there to my own American cousin, Edwin A. Abbey, which is more than I ever did in his native land. In Westminster Abbey Americans abound. Not only are there the bust of Longfellow, the window to Lowell, the tablet to Page, but many lesser men are represented and honored. When one steps outside the door one is confronted with the statue of Lincoln. In front of the National Gallery is a statue of Washington. At St. Saviour's is a bust of John Harvard, an Englishman, but honored thus for his services to America. In the Bodleian Library at Oxford yesterday I found busts of Washington and Franklin. Incidentally, in a number of English histories which I have just been reading, all for English readers and some for English children, the Revolution is treated with such a spirit of fairness and with so little hostility as to raise the question whether the authors have made out as good a case for their ancestors as they well might.

IV

There are some aspects of the personal contact of the two races which, it must be confessed, have unfortunate consequences. As for the appraisal of Americans by the English, the fact that we both speak the same language has its drawbacks. The tongue of every Frenchman, whether gentleman or boor, proclaims his nationality. The best as well as the worst are known for what they are—French. But there is nothing to proclaim so obviously the wellbred, cultivated, quiet-mannered American as American. Unless that fact transpires in some other way, he naturally is considered to be English. On the other hand, there is no mistaking the noisy, underbred American, and, it must be confessed, a most appalling number turn up over here. Nor is it always those without money or apparently any social background who give the English cause to wonder at us as uncultured barbarians. In the quiet English hotel where I always stay in London one is never disturbed by having to overhear the conversation of any English group either in the dining room or in the drawing-rooms. But in every case this winter when an American family has arrived the place has been thrown into a turmoil at once. To cite a specific instance or two: The other day an evidently well-to-do family appeared— father, mother, and son of about fifteen. At dinner the boy came into the dining room ahead of his parents, stood in the middle, and from that vantage point shouted out a conversation to his father, still in the drawing-room, to the con-sternation of the English diners. A few nights afterward another family, evidently of considerable wealth and speaking with an excellent accent, took possession of the drawing-room. The rest of us, quite uninterested, were informed in loud tones of what a new camp in the Adirondacks was like, where the son had been big-game hunting on two continents, and many other personal details, until in despair of being able to read or talk quietly one group of English after another got up and left the room to my fellow citizens. It is evident that this sort of thing does not endear us to the hearts of the quiet and privacy-loving British.

On the other hand, many American tourists, accustomed to the freedom of the Pullman smokers at home and the general atmosphere of Rotarian "glad hand" in America, go back with rankling spirits because the English do not talk to them in railway carriages or hotel lobbies. They do not realize, first, that most Englishmen are shy, and, secondly, that the Englishman, prizing quiet and privacy himself above all else, feels that he has no right to intrude upon others and that, unless obviously called for, it is bad form for him to do so. If, however, he feels justified, or if he thinks he can really be of use to a stranger, not even an American is more ready to make himself agreeable. The other day my wife and I were lost for the moment in some of the winding streets in Chelsea and were studying the map. An Englishwoman at once came up, asked if she could guide us, and walked several blocks to do so. The same thing occurred at Lincoln a few days later.

There is, however, a real fear and dislike of America on the part of some thoughtful people—a reasonable fear and dislike,

I think, based on something far deeper, more subtle, and more important than a war of a hundred and fifty years ago, the precise terms of the debt settlement, or the abominable manners of many American tourists. It is the fear of the Americanization of Europe. For there are many changes going on here and they are not all due to the European situation in itself. What these people fear is not that they are facing years of comparative poverty, of the rise of the new rich, and of the painful reëstablishment of a bad economic situation, but the loss of the ideals and values of what has hitherto constituted their civilization. This the thoughtful traveler also broods over as he sees the changes that have come and the portents of more.

Mass-production in America, the use of advertising to standardize the desires and taste of the public and so standardize production, the consequent lowering of production costs and the increase in wages, have all created a stupendous rise in the scale of American living from the purely material standpoint. With a population of over a hundred millions, undivided by tariff barriers, with most of the raw materials produced at home, with a people singularly lacking in individuality, more than willing to live and have everything exactly like everyone else, the leaders of industry have been able to achieve their ideal of standardized production. But the achievement of this result has brought about the surrender of certain values that the European still thinks of vital importance. What the cultured European desires above all else is to be an individual, to be able to express his own unique personality in work and play. The dreary sameness of American life throughout an entire and vast continent appalls him. Of what use to travel three thousand miles from New York to San Francisco if for the most part one sees only the same sort of people, reads the same comic strips and syndicated news columns, talks the same "shop", and sees the same city architecture?

In Devonshire the other day I was looking from my window at a bit of new garden wall, already beginning to weather and take on beauty in the damp climate. Most skillfully, and without any sense of patchwork, various materials had been put together in it—some gray stone, some of the red Devon sandstone, concrete, and different sorts of brick, with the effect of variety and interest. An American might have done if more "efficiently" of one material, but then no one would have cared to give it a second glance. The old cottages also gain much of their charm from the variety of materials employed—brick, old oak, stucco, shingles, and clapboards. That evening I happened to read that the American Department of Commerce, coöperating with manufacturers in the interests of "efficiency," had reduced the varieties of bricks to be produced from sixty-six to seven, two hundred and ten different shapes of bottles to twenty, and so on, and that the suggestions had been received "with enthusiasm." Nothing could better display the difference in the ideals of the two countries. After all, if we are all to have more and more things, but only on the condition that they shall be exactly like everyone else's, what becomes of the joy of individual living, of expressing your own personality—provided you have one—in work and play? Is it worth while to gain the whole material world and lose your own soul?

America, overwhelmed like a child on Christmas morning with all its new toys, does not yet seem to give a thought as to where it is all going to end. The average business man resents as almost impious, certainly "unpatriotic," any suggestion that all is not for the best, so long as his profits pile up annually. If anyone tries to discuss soberly the possible pitfalls of present tendencies, he is apt to have thrown at him, even by university men at home, some such remark as "Get over your grouch" or "America has no place for kickers," for the average business man, though he takes himself most seriously, is incredibly naive and immature. The average American, so far from resenting the fact that Big Business is out to limit his choice of things more and more while increasing their number, that it is utilizing all the resources of science in psychological advertising to train him to submerge his individuality in order to simplify business for the manufacturer, to make him a mere "consumer" and not a man, seems to welcome it. In itself that is a sign of immaturity. The schoolboy above all else dreads being "different." It is only as one grows to maturity that he insists on being himself and expressing himself in his own way.

Europe is mature if it is poor. It has come to know that there are better values in life than a host of material conveniences and possessions. But it *is* poor. It owes to America the greatest money debt that the world has ever dreamed of. America, with its vast resources, its boiling prosperity, half of the world's gold, is sucking Europe into the maelstrom of its own whirling industrial life. Europe feels itself slipping against its will, and clings desperately to the shore. It is possible that the present economic régime in America cannot last forever. When overproduction gluts the home market, when manufacturers have to enter into foreign competition for new markets, the story may be different, though the time may be far off. But in the mean time what may happen to the older and the more civilized ideals of the value of individuality and craftsmanship and artistic products?

Even now we have to go to Europe for such things as require individual talent. We still have brains and skill at the top, but are killing them off at the bottom. During the war we had to get Austrians to make our maps because there were no skilled American draftsmen for the work. In one of the finest churches in America the architect designed the carved stone—though in the Middle Ages the workmen would do that themselves—and then had to import workmen from Italy to execute it. Meanwhile Europe owes the debts and we insist they must be paid. The masses heavily taxed look toward American prosperity and methods. Here and there mass production is being tried, although Europe, with its limited and highly differentiated markets, can never fully compete. It is not, as many Americans think, merely a matter of national jealousies or tariff barriers, but of an individualism that makes the world more interesting and richer.

If Europe is sucked into the whirlpool, if her form of civilization gives way to the American, and if we are at last world-standardized to one bottle and one brick and one dress and one bath and one car and one book and one idea, it may be that we shall regret the day when every Englishman could pride himself on being singular and "a little mad." And so one wonders as one walks about this old city of London—where tulips and irises dot lawns of inestimable "real estate" value, where one feels a complete liberty to express one's individuality, where one is not limited to one brick in seven or one bottle in twenty, where one feels complete personal liberty within a framework of reasonable and observed law—how long it will last; and, if from poverty and the pressure of American gold it all falls to the low level of American efficiency, mass production, and controlled and standardized lives, what one will do for ideas and ideals and all the possible varied interest and charm of human life. It is not impossible that the world of men may eventually be infinitely poorer because of our colossal and unthinking prosperity.

CHAPTER XIII
THE ART OF LIVING

THE ART OF LIVING

It is an easy phrase, "the art of living," and one which, like any cliché, is rather of the tongue than of the mind, yet in a general way we know well enough what we mean to signify by it. It means primarily an intelligent ordering of experience, and, to that end, an intelligent ordering of the relations between ourselves and the outer world of things or the inner world of possible emotions and thoughts. As one moves about the world in order to test life in its great foci, in New York or Washington, London or Paris, Prague or Vienna, one cannot but be struck by the differing degrees in which various peoples have attained to the practice of this most difficult of all the arts. In America, indeed, there seems to be hardly any appreciation at all on the part of most people that such an art exists. Any discussion of it is relegated by them to that sphere of nonsensical moonshine that may be indulged in by billionaires or by those inefficient Europeans who do not realize that time is money. It is not without significance that in Europe the ordering of our existence is spoken of as "the art of life," whereas when any such discussion takes place in America it is usually under the caption, "the business of life."

There is, of course, a business of life. A man must have some financial means of support; he must have some sort of shelter; some sort of clothing; he must put a certain amount of food into his body daily. The business of life, however, is much the same for man as it is for the animals,

[289]

although it may be more complicated. It is only when man attempts to rise above the mere business of life, and order the experiences of his life, that he becomes man. An architect cannot do without bricks and steel, but the workman who spends his life puddling molten steel in the furnace or putting clay in the ovens is not an architect. Machines will some day do the work as well, but no machine will ever design a cathedral of Amiens, arrange the glass in a rose window of Chartres or daringly raise the choir at Beauvais. Just as the art of building is utterly different from the business of building, so does the art of life differ from the business of life. The difference extends throughout the whole domain of experience. It is not concerned merely with the highbrow. Eating at a lunch counter in New York belongs to the business of life; eating at a café in France belongs to the art of life; though one may put as many calories into one's body in the one as in the other.

The primary concern of every artist of every sort must be a vision of that to which he would attain, of that which he would make. The sculptor sees the finished statue before he begins to mould the clay; the painter sees his picture before he adds touch to touch of color upon his canvas; the poet knows what he would say before he begins to weave the magic of his words; and the composer has heard his symphony before he struggles with the writing of his notes. Obviously, if there is a parallel art of living, the artist in life must have some conception of his finished product, of what sort of life he is trying to make.

For any artist, again, there are the materials and tools with which he works, and just as the material of the musician is sound, that of the sculptor marble or bronze, that of the poet words, so the material with which the artist in life deals must be thought and emotion, using the terms in their very widest senses. The range of these is practically unlimited, infinitely more so than the materials available to any other artist. So again we find a far more varied assortment among what we may call the tools with which the artist in life may work as compared with those of other artists.

Any art is circumscribed by its technique. Marble must be chiselled with a limited number of tools in certain ways, sound must be produced by a similarly limited number of instruments, and so in the other arts. But the artist in life is confronted by an almost infinite number of "tools" which for him consist of all those things by which thought and emotion can be brought into being. For example, he has the finished product of every other art—statues, poems, music, paintings. There is also the whole world of practical appliances—houses, clothes, automobiles, money, telephones, all the innumerable contrivances for man's comfort or ostentation. There are, further, the endless forms of activity of work or play—business, the professions, travel, sport. There are the individualized relationships of parenthood, acquaintance, friendship, love. In a word, everything, tangible and intangible, is a "tool" with which the artist in life may produce thought or emotion, and so modify the life itself conceived as a product of art. It is evident that whoever would practice an art of living is likely to be overwhelmed by the wealth of his material and by the unlimited choice of tools with which to mould it into specific forms.

For centuries past the problem for professing Christians at least was theoretically simple. This life did not count at all save as a preparation for an eternal one, entrance to the happiness of which was possible only by following certain rules of conduct. Today, however, the problem for most people is what is the most perfect or satisfying life for our few years on earth, with no fixed rules to guide. Just as the breaking down of so many barriers of thought at the time of the Renaissance freed all the other arts and allowed them to flower, so the breaking down of barriers today would seem to give the art of life its opportunity as never before. As far as the tyranny of old ideas is concerned we are freer than at any other period of history to order our lives according to art. Moreover, we have infinitely more tools to do it with. They are being thrust into our hands with amazing rapidity, though we play with them without thinking what we are doing or making. The result, it must be confessed, is a haphazard existence instead of an art of living.

Indeed, it may be asked if this sudden wealth of new tools has not overwhelmed us. Are not most of us in the position of being provided with undreamed-of resources for an artist but with no ideas and no technique? It is a platitude to say that we are at the beginning of a new era facing a wholly altered world. If there is no art of living, then all we can do is to bungle along. But if there is any such art, then evidently the first thing of all is to decide what we want to make, what sort of life is worth while, what sort of thoughts and emotions. What with the lack of time, the pressure of community opinion and the insistence of standardized advertising, most of us take the easiest way by thinking that what we want is what our neighbors have. But just as standardized machine production has killed the arts of the old crafts, so standardized living quickly kills any art of living.

If there can be any art of living, any ordering of life to yield us the richest and deepest experiences from this strange adventure into self-consciousness, it is evident that the individual has got to decide what for him or her are the abiding values in life. As it is, our minds are apt to be like the first page of a newspaper in which a home run by Babe Ruth may get the same space as the fall of an empire. If we stopped to consider sanely what for each of us are the real values in life, ranging them in order of significance and importance for *us*, might not many of us find that they do not consist at all in the things we are striving for? Might we not throw away many of the tools which everyone is using thoughtlessly and habitually merely because everyone else is? We would have seen that they do not produce any such thought or emotion as should fit into that unique production which is our own individual life. For one of the fundamental differences between a work of art and a machine product is that the former is unique. All art involves a selection according to a scale of values. The camera may render the total detail of a landscape with more exactitude than a painter, but the latter selects the details and then through his technique and his own personality he produces a work of art which has a unique and artistic quality.

Is it, perhaps, that the material for an art of life is so vast and our tools have become so numerous that there is no possibility of an artistic ordering of our experience? Has it all become too complex and are we reduced to a chaotic and disordered succession of thoughts and emotions? If not, then the artist in life must do just as any other does, learn his technique of production, the proper use of his tools and material to produce a definite result at which he aims, and rigidly reject all which does not contribute to the one work of art of which he has seen the vision.

That is, perhaps, one of the greatest difficulties in the way of an art of life in America. We mix up our money and motor cars and relationships and all the rest of our "tools" as thoughtlessly as a painter might squeeze all his tubes of color onto his canvas, and we get as a result the same sort of daub, in terms of life. Or we are like children striking the notes of a piano at random and achieving the same jangle in life that they do in sound. We select and reject mainly as governed by income. We do so because we have no scale of values, and we have no values because we have no idea what sort of life we really wish to live to express our individuality.

But we cannot select unless we can place comparative values on the various things life offers us, and we cannot value them unless we have arrived at some *standard* of value. The only standard is what we consider a worthwhile life for each of us individually. For various reasons the tyranny of crowd opinion has always been greater in America than in most civilized countries, but it is, of course, one of the great dangers of democracy everywhere. Many people seem to believe that the life of the savage is one of delightful independence, of doing what suits himself all day long. No idea could be further from the truth. The savage is hemmed and circumscribed at almost every point in his personal life by the *mores* of his tribe. Liberty, freedom of speech and action, the right and opportunity for free self-expression, are among the highest products of civilization, not of savagery, and the belief that the reverse is the case is merely an example of the present day tendency to exalt the ideal of savagery and to return on our tracks, evident in all the arts.

Democracy, a certain weariness of the complexities of that very process of civilization that has made freedom possible, and the misunderstood teachings of scientific research, all three are tending to make the tyranny of the crowd greater and an art of life more difficult. In a recent American prize contest for definitions of morality, for example, one of the three which won prizes was as follows: "Morality is that form of human behavior conceded to be virtuous by the conventions of the group to which the individual belongs," and we are told that among all the definitions submitted there was little disagreement as to the general concept. Of course this is the muddiest sort of thinking. The particular social forms which morality takes among the crowd at any given time is confused with morality itself, and, if the definition were true, any advance in moral concepts on the part of either society or the individual would become impossible, as no society ever changed its "moral" opinions unanimously overnight. That such a definition should have become the general one in America is merely an interesting example of the difficulty amongst us of disentangling one's individual self from the glutinous mass of all one's compatriots and fellow Rotarians and Christian Endeavorers.

To practise an art of living it is essential, as I have said, to arrive at some standard of values for ourselves. If we may judge from this contest, and from other evidences, the standard of value arrived at by the American people in the broad sphere of ethics or morality is merely the standard of what the overwhelming mass of Americans of all sorts consider applicable to themselves. There can be no individuality in conforming to such a standard so arrived at. Moreover, such a standard is bound to be beastly low. The mass of men has never risen without individuals to make it rise any more than a mass of dough will rise without the tiny bit of yeast in it. Our concern here, however, is with the individual who would manage his life with art, not with the mass, and for him no art of life is possible if he is merely going to make his life conform to the opinions of the majority. It is as absurd as it would be to think of Keats, preparing to write an "Ode to a Nightingale," taking a vote of all his fellow apothecary apprentices as to what they thought he ought to say about a nightingale.

But we have also got to consider carefully what tools to use in our art. Limiting ourselves for the moment to what are usually called "things," it is obvious, though generally overlooked, that the effect upon ourselves of "things" is both varied and profound. This is a theme which is rarely treated, but the reader will recall the effect upon Lee Randon of the French doll on his mantelpiece in Hergesheimer's "Cytherea." It is, perhaps, the best illustration I can offer of the idea worked out to its conclusion in all completeness. The other day I happened to be visiting the exhibition of the *Arts Decoratifs* at the *Grand Palais* in Paris. The new art in France, and elsewhere over here in Europe, is producing a wholly new form of interior decoration and furnishing, sometimes of great beauty and nearly always of much interest. As I stood in one bedroom in which the bed of ivory and ebony of indescribable design had its covering of leopard skins, I could not help musing on what subtle differences in one's spiritual and intellectual character would come from living one's life amid such furnishings, as contrasted, we will

[296]

say, with bedrooms of complete and perfect Queen Anne or Louis Quatorze. In the room I mention, the atmosphere, due to the furnishing, was an almost maleficent blending of the perfection of twentieth century civilization with the savagery of the jungle. As one stood there, in a room designed as the last word in French art and craftsmanship for a millionaire of 1929, one was aware in part of one's soul of the faint booming of tom-toms and of the odor of black and sweaty jungle flesh. A man could not live in that room without strange things happening in the depths of his being.

This, perhaps, may be said to be an extreme example, as was Hergesheimer's, but is it? Do not all our surroundings and things affect us? The social effects of such things as automobiles, radios and so on have now become commonplaces, but what of the effects on the individual? In many ways a man or woman with a motor car is a different creature from one without one. Think how many lives have been altered by the reading of a single book. The laboring man who lives in a Sixth Avenue room in New York facing on the elevated railroad is a different man from one who lives in a cottage and garden in Devon or amid quiet and roses in the Vaucluse. All this would seem to be so self-evident as to call for no elaboration, and yet do we pay any attention to it? When we try to live as everyone else does, when we buy something because "everybody has one," are we not using our tools with an utter lack of discrimination? There is a similar decadence in some directions in the arts other than that of life, a tendency to put "any old thing" on canvas, to clutter up a novel with irrelevant details on the plea of realism. We might as well try to eat everything as have everything, regardless of our own taste or the idiosyncrasies of our own digestions. A painter does not use his scarlet or blue or orange brushes regardless of the effect, merely because they are "there." He selects his colors as he does his objects, for their final influence on his work, or he merely produces a daub. If we are to have an art of life, must we not exercise equal care in trying to discriminate between the influences and values of all the tools that we use in making the infinitely more complex work, an individual human life of significance and happiness and worth? We have got to think what all these tools—things, situations, surroundings, relationships—may mean for our own individual selves, for our own private lives, regardless of the standards of the majority, before we can begin to live as human beings and develop an art of life. Otherwise we are mere telephone switchboards, like animals, receiving stimuli and sending out reactions.

Until we have given thought to this, we can use all our tools and material only at random and with no idea of the result we are producing. If we can decide what we want to make of ourselves and what tools will best assist the result, then we can vastly simplify our lives by a wholesale rejection of all those things which may be well enough for our neighbors but do not conduce to the one desired end for ourselves. We would then no longer wear ourselves out in the mere living of standardized lives and keeping up with the Joneses. We would not only simplify our lives but we would introduce variety into the deadly monotony of the national life. No two artists would have exactly the same conception of a subject or treat it in exactly the same way.

If it is true that our lives are increasingly frustrate and commonplace and standardized because we do not take time and trouble to think out what is the worthwhile life and achieve a scale of values is it not because we lack the courage to be different from the Joneses and to give to our lives that precise quality of uniqueness which is characteristic of the products of art?

The three qualities, therefore, which would seem to be essential to any artistic ordering of our lives are courage, thought and will. We have got to acquire that rarest form of courage in America, the courage to be considered different from our neighbors and the rest of our set.

If Mrs. Jones's greatest joys in life are the perfectly appointed dinners she delights in being known to give, and riding in her Rolls-Royce, then let her have them if she can afford them. But if your greatest joys are simple hospitality and the good talk around the board, and if you care far more for books than the sort of car that affords you transportation, then in the name of Art give simple dinners, line your shelves with books and drive a Ford.

If you love Elizabethan drama and detest the current fiction, read your drama; and when someone asks you if you have read *The Mauve Petticoat*, tell him candidly that you have not and that you do not intend to. If you are intelligent enough to be bored stiff with the absurd social life of ninety-nine clubs in a hundred, refuse to join the things and amuse yourself in your own way.

Americans pride themselves on their courage and individuality and brag of the frontier virtues, but the fact is we are the most cowardly race in the world socially. Read Emerson's essay on *Self Reliance* and ask yourself honestly how much you dare to be yourself. He has been called the most essentially American of our authors, but would he be so today? The old phrases have a familiar ring. "Trust thyself: every heart vibrates to that iron string." "Whoso would be a man must be a nonconformist." "My life is not an apology, but a life. It is for itself and not for a spectacle." "What I must do is all that concerns me, not what the people think." "Life only avails, not the having lived." "Insist on yourself; never imitate." Every schoolboy knows them, but how many mature Americans dare to practise them? Take the matter of clothes as a simple touchstone of individuality. Every American woman who goes to London is either shocked, interested or amused by the variety of women's dress there. Most of it, except sports clothes, is, I admit, extremely bad, but the point is that a woman dresses just as she pleases. Little girls may have long black stockings or legs bare to their full length; older women may have skirts that display the knee or drag the ground; hats of the latest mode from Paris, or from Regent Street when Victoria was a girl. Watching the passing crowd on the Broad Walk is like turning the pages of Punch for half a century. A man may wear any headgear from a golf cap to a pearl satin "topper." Compare this, for example, with New York and the mass antics of the Stock Exchange where if a man wears a straw hat beyond the day appointed by his fellows they smash it down over his eyes, and where he is not safe from similar moronic hoodlumism even in the streets. I mention clothes not as a *Sartor Resartus* but merely as a simple instance of that mass-mindedness which permeates all American life. One has to fight to be one's self in America as in no other country I know. Not only are most Americans anxious to conform to the standards of the majority, but that majority, and the advertisers, insist that they shall.

I recall some years ago when living in a small village and when I was spending many hundreds of dollars more than I could well afford on books and also putting money into travel, that more than one of the village people actually suggested to me that it was rather disgraceful for a man in my position not to drive a better car than a Ford. My answer, of course, was that I did not give a rap about a car except as a means to get about, and I did care about books and travel. Another man, one from the city, speaking of the same sore point, said that *I* could afford to use a Ford because everyone knew who my grandfather was, but *he* had to have something better to meet his guests with. In another community, a moderately wealthy friend of mine who had a large house, also a country place, and did a good deal of traveling, was taken to task by a yet wealthier neighbor on the score that, again, "a man in his position" owed it to his wife to give her a better car than a Dodge sedan to make calls in, though both my friend and the wife preferred to spend their money in other ways than in running a Packard or a Cadillac. Spending one's money in one's own way in America—that is, trying to use the tools of life with sanity and discrimination— is a good deal like running the old Indian gauntlet. The self-appointed monitors of society to tell other people how they should live, ran, in the cases above, all the way from village store-keepers to a successful New York business man worth many millions, but they are merely typical of that pressure, express or implied, that is brought to bear on any individual who attempts to think out and live his own life. But if our lives are to be based on any art of living, if our souls are not to be suppressed and submerged under a vast heap of standardized plumbing, motor cars, crack schools for the children, suburban social standards and customs, fear of group opinion, and all the rest of our *mores* and taboos, then the first and most essential factor is courage, the simple courage to do what you really want to do with your own life.

But if courage, especially in America, is essential to an art of living, thought is fundamental. A man has got to think out what sort of life he really wants, what life he is going to try to make for himself. If he refuses to face that problem and merely drifts, he abandons himself to the mould that his neighbors provide for him. He will become both for himself and others the utterly uninteresting nonentity that so many Americans are, simply because they have taken the line of least resistance and become mere replicas of thousands of their fellows. When you have seen one Ford car turned out any year, you have seen the whole four million, or whatever the number is. They may be very good and very useful and very sturdy, but they cannot have the slightest interest as individual specimens for anyone.

You will not find it so easy a task as you may think to decide what sort of life you really do want to make. To do so requires a clear mind, independent thinking, and a knowledge of what the infinite variety of goods and values in life are. Most people dream idly a good deal of what they might like but few have either the ability or power to think through what they really do want, given all the conditions of their own selves and their possibilities. It is not only the young girl who does not know what she wants, who dreams one day of becoming an author because "it must be thrilling to live in Greenwich Village and talk to real writers," and another of becoming a clerk in a store because "it must be wonderful to feel you are really *doing* something." The hardheaded business man who has fought his way up from a shoestring to millions, knows often just as little what he wants, as any number of rich men bored to death with power and leisure can testify. Perhaps as useful a task of education as any would be to teach young people what the possibilities of life are.

It may as well be confessed that most people cannot become artists in living. That is not snobbery. It is simple truth. The day may come, if democracy insists on continuing to debase all our spiritual coinage, when anyone may aspire to call himself a poet or a musician or a sculptor. However, that won't make him one. There is no more reason to expect that anyone can be a genuine artist in life than to expect everyone to be an artist in words or sounds or colors. If we all cannot aspire to become great artists of any sort, however, there is happily room for us as amateurs in any art, if we care about it; and our own happiness, as well as our interest for others, is greatly increased by trying to express, in any art, our own individuality. The other arts are merely tools for the great all-embracing art, that of living, and we cannot refuse to become amateurs in that art without confession of failure as civilized beings. If all this complex, delicate, and, it may as well be confessed, burdensome thing we call civilization is merely to be used to make us more intricate switch-boards of automatic stimuli and reactions, then we might as well smash it and be done with it. Its only excuse is in increasing our liberty of choice, our chance to be more individual among a wider range of goods than can the savage or the barbarian.

Moreover, if one would practise the art of living, he must have the artistic spirit. I do not mean the aesthetic in its narrower meaning, but the spirit of the man who finds joy in his own creating of something beautiful or noble or lovely. Life, as Emerson says, must be for itself and not for a spectacle. Artists may get great pay for their work, but if they have spent their lives with their minds on the pay and not on the work, they have not been artists. It is the work, indeed the working, that counts and that is its own best reward. Nor must we defer the practice of our art. A poet or a painter or a musician does not say to himself, "I will make a million first, and then I will write poetry or paint pictures or compose music." His art is life itself, the best of life, for the genuine artist. Money and freedom may be pleasant and useful but they are not the essence of any art, that of life any more than any other. Keats did not postpone writing his poetry until he could retire from mixing drugs and find a cottage in the country. If he had, there would have been no poetry to make his name immortal. And if anyone says of the art of life, that he will try to order his life artistically when he has another five thousand a year, or when he is vice-president instead of sales manager or when he can quit, he will never so order it at all. He does not understand and has not got it in him. He will simply take his place in the American procession with the other four million Fords of the year.

If you decide that you have the courage to "be different," if you can decide what you really want of life, then you may achieve an art of living if you have the will to see it through. And you will find, incidentally, that in place of the sheep-like flocks of country-club Joneses you will have as friends and guests a far more interesting group, that your life will have attained to a depth and a richness of experience that is denied to the standardized Joneses and all their kith and kin, and that you are no longer an automaton with inhibitions but a human being expressing your own unique personality: loving, enjoying, experiencing, suffering perhaps, but *alive.* Your life will not be a machine-made product identical with millions of others turned out by the same firm, but a work of art which will give joy to yourself and others because it is like no other.

But if you merely settle down, unthinkingly and un-courageously, in the mould provided for you by your neigh-bors, if you accept as standards and values merely those of the majority, you will not be an individual or even the useful citizen you may think yourself though you attend every meeting of your association in the year. America can count such men, as she can her motor cars, by the tens of millions. What she needs as useful citizens today are men and women who dare to be themselves, who know with Emerson that "life only avails, not the having lived," who can conceive how rich and varied life can be, and who, with the spirit of the artist and at least an amateur's knowledge of tools and technique, will defy the crowd and show what an art of living may be. Americans have never lacked courage on the fields of battle. It is time they showed some on the golf links. We are more afraid of what our best customer may think or what Mrs. Umpty Bullmarket-Jones may say than our ancestors ever were of what the redskins might do. If I thought mottoes and slogans did any good, I would replace the "God bless our happy home" of a generation or two ago, and the "say it quick" of our offices today, with old Emerson's "Be yourself." That is what every artist, every civilized man and woman has got to be, as the very foundation of an

[305]

art of living. It is, indeed, only the foundation but it is essential. Every art is social. It is the result of a relation between the artist and his time. Music could not have developed as a result of a succession of individual musicians composing for a society of the deaf, and before we can develop an art of living in America and adjust our machinery of life to its practice as it is adjusted in many ways in Europe, we must develop a taste for individual living in thousands of Americans who will refuse to bow the knee to the crowd, whether city, suburban or village, and insist upon being themselves. The road of conformity is merely the road back to savagery.

BONIBOOKS

Here is a list of books of solid and enduring literary value. With the addition, from time to time, of new titles, the publishers pride themselves that they have achieved their aim of making the Bonibooks' imprint synonymous with literary and intrinsic excellence. The books are attractive in appearance, with a sturdy full-cloth binding, stamped in silver, printed on paper of good quality. $1.00 each.